Collins need to

Zodiac types

INNISFIL PUBLIC LIBRARY
P.O. BOX 7049
INNISFIL, ON L9S 1A8

All the information you need
to analyse friends, family and yourself

133.52 Sto

Th Stokes, J.   P
Zodiac types.

PRICE: $12.37 (3710/an/ch)

First published in 2004 by
Collins, an imprint of
HarperCollins*Publishers*
77-85 Fulham Palace Road
Hammersmith, London W6 8JB

The Collins website address is:
www.collins.co.uk

Collins is a registered trademark of HarperCollins Publishers Limited.

08 07 06 05 04
6   5   4   3   2   1

Text and illustrations © Diagram Visual Information Ltd, 2004
Design © HarperCollins*Publishers*, 2004

All rights reserved. No part of this publication may be reproduced,
stored in a retrieval system, or transmitted, in any form or by any
means, electronic, mechanical, photocopying, recording or otherwise,
without the prior written permission of the publishers.

A catalogue record for this book is available from the British Library

Author: Jamie Stokes
Editors: Gordon Lee, Howard Loxton
Production: Richard Hummerstone, Lee Lawrence, Chris Owens, Tony Atherton
Research: Neil McKenna
Picture credits: Biblioteca Estense, Modena pp. 18–19, 32–33, 46–47, 60–61,
    74–75, 88–89, 102–103, 116–117, 130–131, 145–146, 158–159, 172–173.
    Robert Opie Collection pp. 31, 59
    Neil McKenna Collection pp. 17, 24, 31, 38, 45, 52, 66, 73, 80, 87, 94, 101,
    108, 115, 122, 129, 136, 143, 150, 157, 164, 171, 178.
Cover design: Cook Design
Front cover photograph: Henrik Sorensen/Getty Images

ISBN 0 00 718038 1

Colour reproduction by Colourscan, Singapore
Printed and bound by Printing Express Ltd, Hong Kong

contents

Introduction

Collins need to know? Zodiac types is a fun and informative look at what the zodiac can tell you about your character, and the characters of friends, lovers and celebrities. You will find information about the way people born under each sign approach life, love, sex, money, food, work and their homes, as well as how to spot the tell-tale signs of each zodiac type.

Zodiac signs defined

Almost everybody knows what their 'sign' is, even if they deny that it has any significance. Far fewer people know exactly why being born between two apparently random dates in the year should make you, for example, a Capricorn. The answer lies in the movement of the Sun. When viewed from the Earth, the Sun, the Moon and all the planets move across the sky within a surprisingly narrow band. This band is known to astrologers as the zodiac, and it can be pictured as a vast, imaginary pathway that stretches across the sky from one horizon to the other. This pathway passes all the way around the Earth: it is a circle, and is therefore made up of 360 degrees.

Thousands of years ago, astrologers divided this band into twelve exactly equal segments. Each segment is a zodiac sign and is named after a significant constellation of stars. As everybody knows, the Sun's position in the sky changes throughout the year, which means that the Sun passes through each of the twelve zodiac signs on the band once each year. This pattern of movement is fixed, so the Sun always moves out of one sign and into the next at the same time every year.

Your zodiac sign, or 'star sign' if you prefer, is the sign that the Sun happens to be occupying at the time of your birth. Professional astrologers would call this your Sun-sign, for obvious reasons. Your Sun-sign has a strong bearing on basic elements of your character, but it is not the whole story. When you were born, all of the other planets were scattered in various positions throughout the zodiac too. When compiling a full birth chart, astrologers consider the positions of all of the planets. However, this book is only concerned with Sun-signs.

Understanding the basics of Sun-sign astrology can change the way you look at everybody you encounter, from the most intimate of partners to the most fleeting acquaintance. It offers a fascinating insight into the hidden yearnings and fears that motivate all of us.

Birth charts

Many people complain that they are nothing like what their Sun-sign says they should be. This is often due to the powerful influence of the other planets. The chart below is a standard birth chart for a person born on 25 May, 1931. Any astrology book will tell you that this makes them a Gemini (the Sun symbol is shown in Gemini on the chart). However, the birth chart also shows that the Moon, ruler of the emotions, was in Virgo at the time of birth. Emotionally, this person is likely to exhibit the Virgoan characteristic of fussiness rather than the Geminian characteristic of detachment.

In this chart none of the other planets are in Gemini, so there are probably quite a few areas in which this person's character differs from the classic description of a Gemini. The Sun-sign character traits detailed in this book provide a broad outline of a person's motivations, tastes and fears. For a fully comprehensive birth chart, you will need to consult a professional astrologer, or learn how to draw one up yourself.

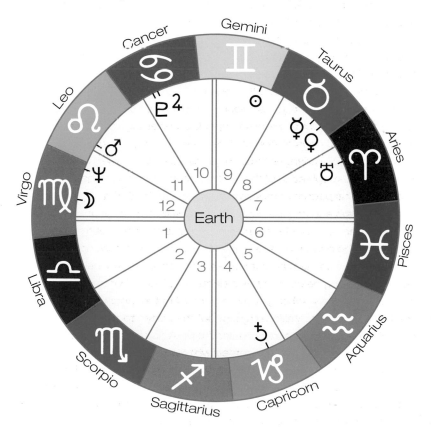

Use this table to find your Sun-sign:

Sign	Dates
Aries	21 March–19 April
Taurus	20 April–20 May
Gemini	21 May–20 June
Cancer	21 June–22 July
Leo	23 July–22 August
Virgo	23 August–22 September
Libra	23 September–22 October
Scorpio	23 October–21 November
Sagittarius	22 November–21 December
Capricorn	22 December–19 January
Aquarius	20 January–18 Febuary
Pisces	19 February–20 March

Are you sure about your Sun-sign?

Tables such as the one above are approximations that give the correct answer most of the time. The Sun passes through the 360 degrees of the zodiac once a year, but a year is 365 days long. The slight discrepancy between these numbers means that finding your Sun-sign is not as simple as you may have been led to believe. The actual day on which the Sun moves from any one sign into the next can differ from year to year. The charts starting on page 182 of this book will tell you when each transition took place for every year from 1931 to the present.

The cusp

If your birthday falls on the first or last day of your particular sign, you may have been told that you were born 'on the cusp' and that you will have characteristics of both signs. No professional astrologer would agree. You are either one sign or the other, no matter how close to the boundary you were born. This is why it is important to track down your actual Sun-sign. Unless you are sure which sign you were actually born under, nothing else that astrology has to say about you will make sense.

Astrological predictions

The astrology covered in this book deals strictly with the influence of the Sun on the character of an individual. Astrologers examine the positions of all of the planets when preparing detailed birth charts, which can then be used to predict a person's future. This is done by superimposing the positions of the planets at a future date onto the birth chart, and interpreting the way that they relate to each other. If you find the information in this book revealing, you may be tempted to look into the subject further. The section at the end of this book entitled **Need to know more?** (page 190) shows you where to go if you want to find out more about the almost infinite subtleties of astrology.

Astrology and free will

Some people object to astrology because they feel that it undermines the concept of free will. Reputable astrologers never claim that, just because you happen to be born when a particular planet was in a particular position, they can predict what you will do in any given situation. All they can say is that you are likely to have certain characteristics. For example, Geminis have a tendency to be indecisive, but the same characteristic also makes them quick and flexible thinkers. All the traits attributed to the different signs have this dual quality: they can be beneficial or detrimental depending on the situation.

How to use this book

Astrology is a huge subject and the space in this book is limited. Nevertheless, even the basics of Sun-sign analysis can provide startling insights into your own character and the characters of those close to you. You can't expect every Libran you know to behave exactly as Librans are described in this book but, if you look more closely, you will probably find that they do have common motivations and tendencies that you may never have noticed before. Bear the following points in mind:

- There is no such thing as an exemplary Leo or Capricorn etc.; the planets always introduce subtle variations.
- People often try to conceal their true motivations.
- Even negative characteristics might not show up in a person's everyday behaviour. We all have free will, which means that we do not always choose to act according to our desires.
- It is possible that a person may have a wrongly-assigned Sun-sign (see the note **Are you sure about your Sun-sign?** on the opposite page).

Astrological terms

air One of the four elements into which the zodiac signs are divided. Air is connected with mental functions.

birth chart A chart used by astrologers to show the positions of the Sun, the Moon and the planets relative to the zodiac signs at the time of a person's birth. Professional astrologers use full birth charts centred on the precise time and geographical location of a person's birth.

cardinal One of the three qualities into which the elements are divided. Cardinal signs are connected with enterprise.

earth One of the four elements into which the zodiac signs are divided. Earth is connected with practicality and materialism.

element Each zodiac sign is assigned to one of the four elements: fire, air, earth and water. The elements represent basic characteristics that are common to the signs they are connected with.

fire One of the four elements into which the zodiac signs are divided. Fire is connected with activity and enthusiasm.

fixed One of the three qualities into which the elements are divided. Fixed signs are connected with stability and determination.

horoscope A birth chart calculated according to the exact time of birth.

mutable One of the three qualities into which the elements are divided. Mutable signs are connected with adaptability and harmonization.

opposite signs The signs exactly opposite each other on the zodiac wheel. Relationships between people with opposite Sun-signs are often complicated; because they have opposing characteristics, they often misunderstand each other's motivations. They can also be complementary, each one bringing something to the relationship that the other lacks. The signs and their opposites are shown in the table below.

Sign	Opposite	Sign	Opposite
Aries	Libra	Cancer	Capricorn
Taurus	Scorpio	Leo	Aquarius
Gemini	Sagittarius	Virgo	Pisces

planets 'Planet' has a specific meaning in astrology since it includes the Sun and the Moon but excludes Earth. The ten astrological planets are: Mercury, Venus, Mars, Jupiter, Saturn, Uranus, Neptune, Pluto, the Moon and the Sun. Each zodiac sign is ruled by one or more planets and the characteristics of the planets are said to influence the character traits of people with those signs. For example Mars, the ruler of Aries, is associated with directness and aggressive energy, both Arien characteristics.

quality Each sign is assigned to one of the four elements, and the three signs connected with each element have one of three qualities. The three qualities are: cardinal, fixed and mutable.

rising sign The sign which is rising above the eastern horizon at the time of a person's birth. It is also known as 'the ascendant'. The rising sign is said to influence the general outlook, appearance, and most obvious personality traits of people born at that time.

ruling planet Each sign is said to be influenced by one or more of the planets, and each planet has specific characteristics. See pages 12–13 for rulers.

star sign A commonly used synonym for 'Sun-sign'.

sun-sign The sign of the zodiac occupied by the Sun on the date of birth. The twelve Sun-signs are Aries, Taurus, Gemini, Cancer, Leo, Virgo, Leo, Scorpio, Sagittarius, Capricorn, Aquarius and Pisces.

water One of the four elements into which the zodiac signs are divided. Water is connected with sensitivity and emotions.

zodiac An imaginary band across the night sky divided into twelve segments of 30 degrees. Each segment corresponds to a sign.

zodiac characteristics Character traits that are determined by the position of the Sun at the time of a person's birth. Very few people have all the character traits associated with their Sun-sign because the positions of the other planets, which can vary widely, also have a strong influence. The descriptions given in this book provide an accurate overview of the main motivations and preoccupations of people born under each sign.

zodiac position All of the planets (including the Sun) move across the sky within a narrow band known to astrologers as the zodiac. The position of a planet is described as being between 0 and 29 degrees 59 minutes within each sign. In the diagram on the following page, the Sun is at about 2 degrees of Capricorn. Planetary positions can be obtained from astronomical tables.

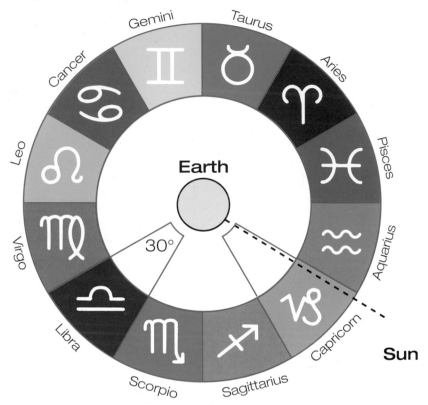

▼ The zodiac band showing the sequence of the zodiac signs.

zodiac signs The zodiac is divided into twelve 30-degree segments, and each segment is a zodiac sign. The segments are named after significant constellations of stars. Because of the motion of the Earth over thousands of years, the constellations are no longer exactly aligned with their zodiac signs as they were when they were first named.

zodiac wheel A representation of the positions of the Sun-signs, relative to each other, in the form of a circle divided into twelve equal segments. Three versions of the zodiac wheel are shown on the opposite page, each one giving different information. The top wheel shows the positions of the twelve Sun-signs; the middle shows which of the elements (air, earth, fire or water) applies to each sign; and the bottom shows which quality (cardinal, fixed or mutable) applies in each case. For example, Aquarius is the eleventh sign. It is preceded by Capricon and succeeded by Pisces. It has the element 'air' and the quality 'fixed', so is the 'fixed air sign'.

ASTROLOGICAL TERMS

10

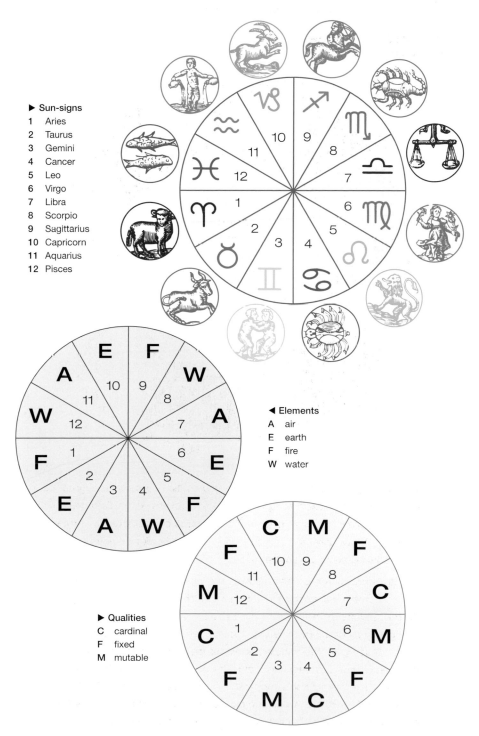

▶ Sun-signs
1 Aries
2 Taurus
3 Gemini
4 Cancer
5 Leo
6 Virgo
7 Libra
8 Scorpio
9 Saglttarius
10 Capricorn
11 Aquarius
12 Pisces

◀ Elements
A air
E earth
F fire
W water

▶ Qualities
C cardinal
F fixed
M mutable

Astrological symbols

The Sun-signs each have a symbol (e.g. the ram for Aries) and a glyph (a pictogram). Astrological glyphs symbolize the essential traits of the Sun-sign that they represent. The glyphs used by astrologers today have their origins in the symbols that were used by philosophers and alchemists thousands of years ago. The planets that rule each sign, and the planets' glyphs, are also shown here.

Sun-sign		Planet
Aries	The Aries glyph represents the horns of the ram, a symbol for the aggressive, forward-pushing character of the sign. It can also be seen as a gushing fountain, a symbol of the irrepressible energy of Aries.	**Mars**
Taurus	This glyph clearly represents the head and horns of the bull; it is very suitable as a symbol for straightforward Taureans. The horns are sometimes seen as a receptive cup instead.	**Venus**
Gemini	A glyph that very closely resembles the Roman numeral two is well suited to Gemini, the sign of the twins and of the spirit of communication between individuals.	**Mercury**
Cancer	A flowing, sensual glyph that primarily represents the claws of the Cancerian crab. The symbol can also be seen as the female breasts and emphasizes the caring, nurturing nature of the Cancerian.	**Moon**
Leo	Another flowing glyph, but this time curving outwards to match Leo's outgoing and energetic character. The sinuous line is also said to represent energy flowing from the Sun.	**Sun**

Sun-sign		Planet

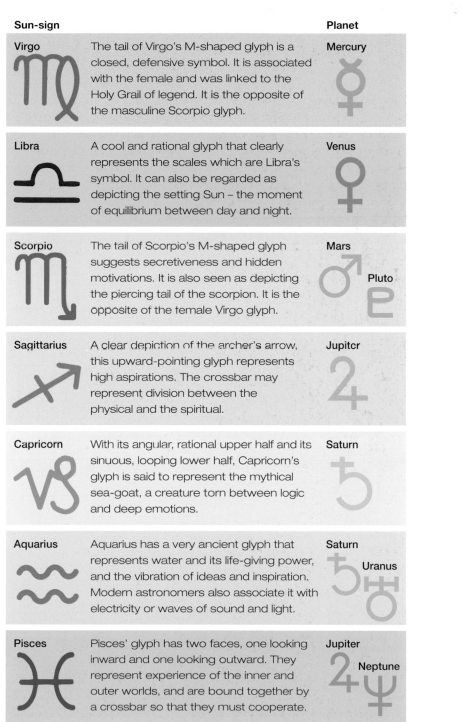

Virgo

The tail of Virgo's M-shaped glyph is a closed, defensive symbol. It is associated with the female and was linked to the Holy Grail of legend. It is the opposite of the masculine Scorpio glyph.

Mercury

Libra

A cool and rational glyph that clearly represents the scales which are Libra's symbol. It can also be regarded as depicting the setting Sun – the moment of equilibrium between day and night.

Venus

Scorpio

The tail of Scorpio's M-shaped glyph suggests secretiveness and hidden motivations. It is also seen as depicting the piercing tail of the scorpion. It is the opposite of the female Virgo glyph.

Mars

Pluto

Sagittarius

A clear depiction of the archer's arrow, this upward-pointing glyph represents high aspirations. The crossbar may represent division between the physical and the spiritual.

Jupiter

Capricorn

With its angular, rational upper half and its sinuous, looping lower half, Capricorn's glyph is said to represent the mythical sea-goat, a creature torn between logic and deep emotions.

Saturn

Aquarius

Aquarius has a very ancient glyph that represents water and its life-giving power, and the vibration of ideas and inspiration. Modern astronomers also associate it with electricity or waves of sound and light.

Saturn

Uranus

Pisces

Pisces' glyph has two faces, one looking inward and one looking outward. They represent experience of the inner and outer worlds, and are bound together by a crossbar so that they must cooperate.

Jupiter

Neptune

ASTROLOGICAL SYMBOLS

13

aries

the ram

21 March–19 April

Key words for Aries, the first sign of the zodiac, are:

- Assertiveness and pioneering
- Challenge and adventure
- Exploration and discovery
- Competition and winning
- Control and nobility
- Courage and openness
- New beginnings

▶ Your element

Aries is the cardinal fire sign. Yours is the pioneer sign of the zodiac, the first of the astrological year, and you are filled with the pioneering spirit. Dynamic, straightforward and tremendously energetic, you forge new trails where others fear to go. Challenge and adventure are your meat and drink, routine and patience are unbearable encumbrances. You burn brightly and you lead from the front.

Your character

▼ Mars, the planet of aggressive energy, rules Aries.

You are a powerhouse of energy and decisiveness. Always on the move, always bursting with the desire to be doing something, you are constantly seeking a challenge worthy of your courageousness and boundless enthusiasm. Unfortunately, not everything in life can be approached effectively with your rocket-powered mentality. You are often accused, not always unfairly, of impatience or using a sledgehammer to crack a nut. In many ways you are like a formula one racing car: absurdly over the top for a trip to the supermarket, but superbly suited to a long-distance, high-speed chase.

Your ruling planet

Mars, planet of the Roman god of war, rules Aries. It makes you a natural and highly successful leader, as long as there is a crisis to be met or a war to be won. It also makes you rather hot-headed and prone to impatience with people who don't share your can-do attitude. You find it very difficult to be conciliatory towards people who don't have the brains to see that you are always right.

Your secrets

It would probably shock most people to know just how important winning or being the brightest and best is to you. Coming first is your prime motivation, not just because you feel that you have to show how much better than everyone else you are, although there's always an element of that, but because it gives you endless opportunities to set yourself goals. Your greatest fear is that you won't be appreciated or liked, even when you are the winner.

CHARACTERISTICS

POSITIVE

- Highly enterprising
- Untiring
- Zest for life
- Courageous pioneer
- Quick-witted
- Easily handle disappointment
- Individualistic
- Fair-minded
- Hard-working

NEGATIVE

- Hot-headed
- Impatient
- Self-centred
- No concept of others' feelings
- Lack of foresight
- Lack of staying power
- Violent temper

LUCKY CONNECTIONS

Colours	Red and white
Plant	Tiger lily
Perfume	Galbanum
Gemstone	Diamond
Metal	Iron
Tarot card	The magician
Animals	Ram and lamb

◀ Doris Day (born 3 April 1924) is one of the few, if not the only, woman to have become a genuine star of film, television, radio and music, a sure sign of sheer Arien drive and ambition in action. Her screen persona, that of a moral, intelligent and unfailingly optimistic woman with the kind of strength of will that made her believable as Calamity Jane, is the epitome of the Arien character.

ARIES

17

The man

These are typical characteristics of the Aries male, but they are by no means universal. Strong influences in an individual's birth chart, such as the positions of the planets, can distort or skew these characteristics, but they are rarely altogether absent.

Typical appearance

- A well-muscled body.
- Noble and energetic bearing.
- Often dresses to impress.
- Blushes easily when emotional.
- Rarely puts on weight.
- Changes little with advancing age.

Personality

- Highly competitive.
- Honest and fair-minded.
- Seizes the initiative.
- A natural leader.
- Tends to brush aside objections.
- Can lose patience with long-term projects.
- Takes risks with money.
- Has a fear of physical disability.
- Puts his partner on a pedestal.

▲ Mars is the ruling planet in both Aries and Scorpio.

YOUNG ARIES

The child

The typical Aries child:

- Endlessly seeks attention.
- Has a tendency to break bones.
- Walks and talks very early.
- Is impossible to put to bed.
- Has almost no fear.
- Tries to dominate other children.
- Is inexhaustibly curious.
- Is very sharing and open.
- Recovers from illness quickly.
- Argues incessantly.

ARIES

The woman

These are typical characteristics of the Aries female, but they are by no means universal. Strong influences in an individual's birth chart, such as the positions of the planets, can distort or skew these characteristics, but they are rarely altogether absent.

Typical appearance

- Slim and strong.
- Has strong and voluminous hair.
- Very energetic and active.
- Likes to wear sophisticated clothes.
- Sometimes has a slightly masculine look.
- Has attractively strong features.
- Aquiline nose and eyebrows.

Personality

- Enthusiastic and optimistic.
- Has no time for weak characters.
- Busy and successful outside the home.
- Open and pathologically honest.
- Has an answer to any problem.
- Very argumentative.
- Is the equal of any man.
- A useful ally and a deadly enemy.

Parenting a young Aries

Simply saying 'no' to an Aries child is unlikely to work. They have a passionate drive to do things their own way and have absolute contempt for other children who are 'goody two-shoes'.

The best way to get an Aries child to do what you want is to make it a challenge. Tell your young Aries that there is no way they can possibly tidy all their toys away in less than five minutes, then step back from the ensuing whirlwind of activity.

Young Ariens need lots of opportunities to show how brave and clever they are. They are likely to be fascinated by games that have a clear winner, but dreadfully bored by cooperative activities. These drives can easily bring them into conflict with other children, so always be ready to provide the emotional reassurance that they pretend they don't need.

▶ Your leisure

LOVES AND HATES

You love
- Being admired.
- Having something that nobody else has.
- Being challenged.
- Being in charge.
- Instant service.

You hate
- Having to wait.
- Having your movements restricted.
- Being ignored.
- Anything bland or out of date.

The phrase 'a change is as good as a rest' is especially true for Ariens. You see leisure time as an ideal opportunity to show how quick and clever you are at something other than your job.

Hobbies and pastimes

Looking for a hobby? Try one of these:
- Competitive sports of any kind.
- Racing cars, bicycles or even tortoises.
- Physically demanding activities with an element of risk.
- Games of strategy.
- Theatre and amateur dramatics.
- Collecting and driving fast and expensive cars.

Your rest

The idea of lounging around by a pool or spending hours sunbathing on the beach fills you with disgust. How could anybody waste so much time doing something so pointless? Show you a pool and you will have organized a water polo game within minutes; show you a beach and you will be yearning to run along it to see how far it goes.

To you, sleep is rest, something you rarely have trouble doing after a day spent rushing around. Daylight hours are far too precious to spend lazing around with your eyes closed. A good meaty project that you can really get your teeth into and see through to a satisfactory conclusion in a fairly short time is your idea of relaxation.

▲ Sports with an element of risk suit Ariens.

▶ Your health

It takes an awful lot to slow an Aries
down. You are very much a physical
being and do whatever you can to
ensure that you retain your customary
healthy vigour.

Sickness

Colds that would floor lesser mortals have
practically no effect on Aries. You can shrug off
the usual sniffles and sneezes, but more serious
illness can lead to depression if it restricts your
ability to be up and about.

You suffer particularly from:

● Fevers.
● Broken bones and other injuries.
● Neuralgia, headaches and migraines.
● Illness of the eyes and ears.
● Sinus trouble.

Body parts linked to Aries

The parts of the body
traditionally linked to
the strong influence
of Aries are as shown
on the right.

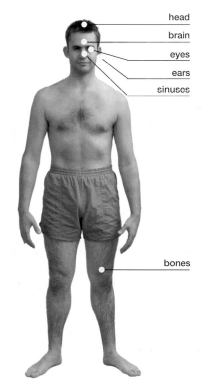

head
brain
eyes
ears
sinuses

bones

▲ A drawing from a
sixteenth-century
calendar shows a
connection between the
Aries and the head of
the human body.

▶ An individual's birth chart
will show if any of these
body parts have inherited a
strength or vulnerability.

ARIES

21

▶ In love

You love the excitement of the chase and can be exceptionally romantic. As with everything else, you have trouble sticking to things long-term. You must ensure that a relationship has challenges if it's going to last.

Falling in love, you:
- Are very direct and a little intimidating.
- Insist on being the pursuer rather than the pursued.
- Place the object of your affection on a pedestal.
- Go all out to impress.
- Are very romantic and old-fashioned.

In love, you expect:
- Absolute fidelity (but not necessarily from yourself!).
- To be admired by your lover.
- Your lover to share your boundless enthusiasm.
- To be constantly busy.
- Your lover to treat you as if you were the only man/woman in the world.

How to capture an Arien's heart
- Be outrageously flirtatious and direct.
- Suggest spur of the moment activities.
- Be prepared to talk about him/her for hours.
- Never whine, beg or be needy.
- Show that you believe in fairness and justice.
- Don't be shy or subtle.

FRIENDSHIPS AT A GLANCE

Check here for personality clashes. Friendship matches are not the same as love matches. Think about it: would you actually want to marry some of your friends?

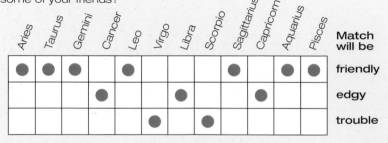

	Aries	Taurus	Gemini	Cancer	Leo	Virgo	Libra	Scorpio	Sagittarius	Capricorn	Aquarius	Pisces	Match will be
	●	●	●		●				●		●	●	friendly
				●			●			●			edgy
						●		●					trouble

ARIES

22

Love matches

Aries
♈
Take a deep breath now, because you're unlikely to have time if you go for this match. Heat and spice guaranteed.

Taurus
♉
Stubborn Taureans could drive you to distraction, but you would never consider it were it not for their seductiveness.

Gemini
♊
Two high-spirited souls with boredom thresholds next to zero. Could be great if you can keep it going long enough.

Cancer
♋
Both have a lot of energy but Cancerians are usually too sensitive to stand bold-as-brass Ariens.

Leo
♌
An awful lot of sparks and heat from these two fire signs. This active, high-spirited match is one of the best.

♥

Virgo
♍
Virgo waits and analyses where Aries leaps in head first. Perhaps you could teach each other a thing or two.

Libra
♎
One of the few cases where opposites really do attract. Spontaneity tempered by balance.

♥

Scorpio
♏
Enough sexual energy to start bushfires, but Ariens are a bit too straightforward for scheming Scorpios.

Sagittarius
♐
Warn innocent bystanders to stand well back. This is one of the classic fire-on-fire, high-energy combinations.

♥

Capricorn
♑
Initial attraction soon turns to frustration when Aries realises that goats are a bit too serious and grown-up.

✘

Aquarius
♒
Aries is a creature of the physical here-and-now, Aquarius of the abstract never-when. Not a good match.

Pisces
♓
A highly risky combination. Aries is nowhere to be seen when Pisces needs spiritual nurturing.

✘

ARIES

23

▶ Sex

Your sexuality is potent, energetic and, like everything else about you, uncompromisingly direct. There aren't many people who can keep up with your rocket-powered libido, but you are more than willing to keep looking.

Your sexuality

Your personality is such that you shine in social situations, so there's never a lack of people who are interested in getting to know you better. On the other hand, your directness can be a bit intimidating, so perhaps you need to learn that not everyone likes to be so open when it comes to sex.

Sexual needs:
- A lover who is sure of what they want.
- A lover who doesn't ask about tomorrow.
- Experimentation and variety.
- To be treated like the most important person in the world.
- Stimulation of all the senses.
- Complete satisfaction, every time.

Sexual turn-ons:
- Initiating a lover into new sexual practices.
- Being totally dominant, or totally passive.
- Exhibitionism and the risk of being caught.
- Making love in the early morning.
- Humour and dirty jokes.
- Vivid fantasies.

Love and sex

You are strongly influenced by the 'grass is always greener' myth. In fact, the only way you are ever going to find true sexual fulfilment is in a long-term loving relationship, because you need the mental closeness that such relationships bring. Eventually, you are going to have to learn to overcome your inner restlessness.

ARIES

24

Famous Ariens

21 Mar	**Marcel Marceau** Mime actor, 22 March 1923
22 Mar	
23 Mar	**Joan Crawford** Actress, 23 March 1908
25 Mar	**Aretha Franklin** Singer, 25 March 1942
26 Mar	
27 Mar	
	Diana Ross Singer, 26 March 1944
30 Mar	**Elton John** Musician, 27 March 1947
	Vincent Van Gogh Painter, 30 March 1853
2 Apr	
3 Apr	**Casanova** Adventurer, 2 April 1725
4 Apr	
	Marlon Brando Actor, 3 April 1924
9 Apr	**Doris Day** Actress, 3 April 1924
	Maya Angelou Writer, 4 April 1928
	Charles-Pierre Baudelaire Poet, 9 April 1821
15 Apr	**Leonardo da Vinci** Artist and inventor, 15 April 1452
16 Apr	
19 Apr	**Charlie Chaplin** Silent film star and director, 16 April 1889

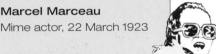

Elton John
(born 27 March 1947)

Vincent Van Gogh
(born 30 March 1853)

Maya Angelou
(born 4 April 1928)

Charles-Pierre
Baudelaire
(born 9 April 1821)

Leonardo da Vinci
(born 15 April 1452)

Charlie Chaplin
(born 16 April 1889)

▶ Everyday life

Home is the place where you feel you must be in total command. Daily life sometimes forces even you to compromise and take orders that you don't like, but inside your own four walls you are absolute sovereign.

Your home

The social set up of your home life is much more important to you than the physical place. You are quite happy to live in either a camper van or a hotel suite, as long as the people you share it with give you the respect you know you deserve, and don't try to put limits on your behaviour. Home is where you let off steam and allow yourself to do exactly as you wish.

Your work

Ariens can be phenomenally useful people to have around, but don't ask them to do anything repetitive.

Job for life?
- Mountaineer or Arctic explorer.
- Politics or public relations.
- Firefighter or police officer.
- Working with metals.
- Circus performer or escapologist.
- Cutting-edge surgeon.
- Any job where the ability to get up early is an advantage.

▲ Ariens (21 March–19 April) are born in the agricultural month of renewing the soil.

Arien boss
- Expects loyalty.
- Has tremendous belief in him/herself.
- Loves to overcome a crisis.
- Can be contradictory.
- Generous with rewards.

Arien worker
- Operates best on his/her own.
- Always seeks promotion.
- Very motivated.
- Easily bored.
- Can be careless with details.
- Needs to be challenged.

Your appetites

All that rushing about that you do requires a lot of fuel. You are almost certainly one of those annoying people who seem able to eat anything at any time without gaining weight.

Theoretically, as a fire sign, you should delight in volcanic vindaloos and the kind of jalapeño peppers that have to be handled with asbestos gloves. A lot of Ariens do in fact like spicy foods, but it isn't a universal trait. More likely is a tendency to indulge in fast foods of every kind. It's very rare that you feel able to spare the time to indulge in something as mundane as preparing a meal. Instant coffee is clearly superior to filter because you don't have to wait around for it. Your microwave oven is rarely idle. You have no objection to elaborate meals, as long as you aren't the one preparing them.

YOUR MONEY AND YOUR FORTUNE

You have a strangely ambivalent attitude towards money; the millionaire lifestyle seems nice, but money itself is so boring. You are much more likely to become rich through a one-off opportunity than a consistent long-term effort. To make your fortune, try these suggestions:

- Get people to sponsor you for an insanely dangerous challenge in a far-away place.
- Open a fast food restaurant and train your staff until they are fast enough to satisfy even you.
- Calculate how long it would take you to earn a million, then do it in half the time.
- Try shopping around rather than buying the first thing you see.
- Start a swear box and put a pound in every time you curse with frustration.
- Get someone to tell you that there is no way you could make more money than Bill Gates.

taurus

the bull

20 April–20 May

Key words for Taurus, the second sign of the zodiac, are:

- Wealth and prosperity
- Beauty and sensuality
- Nature and living things
- Control and dependability
- Organization and tenacity
- Stubbornness and caution
- Strength and kindness

▶ Your element

Taurus is the fixed earth sign. In character, you are a bit like a vast, majestic mountain. You have the solidity and endurance in the face of adversity that you would expect from a soaring peak, as well as a quiet but breathtaking majesty. On the down side, you also tend to move about as fast as a slab of granite and it would probably be easier to move Everest than to get you to change your mind.

Your character

▼ Venus, in her aspect as the queen of sensuality, rules Taurus.

There is a deep-seated paradox in the Taurean character. You are every bit as down-to-earth and tenacious as you would expect from a sign represented by the Bull, but you also have an ethereal and creative side that seems to come from nowhere.

The insatiability of your appetites is legendary, but you are no glutton. Taste and refinement are indelible hallmarks of the Taurean character. You are very strongly anchored in the physical world and this gives you your intuitive sense of style and quality. You can spot a fake, of any kind, at a hundred paces and are completely incapable of deceit.

Your ruling planet

Venus, planet of the love goddess, rules Taurus. Flighty, floaty love might seem incompatible with the plodding reputation of the Bull, but this is a misunderstanding of the nature of Venus. She is the queen of sensuality and lingering luxury rather than tacky kiss-me-quick hats. When you hear that Taureans are down-to-earth, what it really means is that they like to take their shoes and socks off and feel the mud oozing through their toes.

Your secrets

Your two greatest fears are disturbance and poverty. You hate having your routine disturbed, not because you have no imagination but because your routine has been set up to provide you with maximum opportunities for pleasure and aesthetic appreciation. Your fear of poverty is not motivated by a shallow love of cash, but by the fact that you see your very identity as defined by your physical circumstances, and particularly by the quality of the possessions that you love to surround yourself with.

TAURUS

30

Titbits

10p No. 4758
JUNE 2-8, 1977

AUSTRALIA 40c NEW ZEALAND 45c
MALAYSIA 95c SOUTH AFRICA 45c

Shows
the
FLAG

E

...ll-out
...n your
...ndow
...LUS
...our guide
...o the great
...elebration

★ ★   ★ ★

The Hilarious
...REWIND

LUCKY CONNECTIONS

Colours	Pastel shades and blues
Plant	Mallow
Perfume	Storax
Gemstone	Topaz
Metal	Copper
Tarot card	Hierophant (High Priest)
Animal	Bull

CHARACTERISTICS

POSITIVE

- Steady and unflappable
- Unparalleled tenacity
- Highly creative
- Totally trustworthy
- Excellent host
- Supportive and sympathetic friend
- Long-term planner
- Very discriminating
- Careful and reliable

NEGATIVE

- Tendency to moodiness
- Irritatingly stubborn
- Greedy and materialistic
- Slow starter
- Self-indulgent
- Hate novelty or change
- Hides emotions

▲ Queen Elizabeth II (born 21 April 1926) has typical Taurean characteristics. Steadiness and devotion to duty have enabled her to become one of Britain's longest-reigning monarchs, while her down-to-earth sense of morality has ensured she has retained the public's respect throughout these sometimes difficult years.

The man

These are typical characteristics of the Taurean male, but they are by no means universal. Strong influences in an individual's birth chart, such as the positions of the planets, can distort or skew these characteristics, but they are rarely altogether absent.

Typical appearance
- A stocky, muscular physique.
- Very clear, often dark, skin.
- Unruly hair and a fast-growing beard.
- Tendency to plumpness.
- Slow and determined gait.
- Small facial features.

Personality
- Rarely changes his mind.
- Financially very astute.
- Dresses conservatively but expensively.
- Suspicious of new or unusual situations.
- Builds useful social networks.
- Works hard and untiringly.
- Likely to have musical or artistic talent.
- Loves the outdoors.
- Forms few, but deep, relationships.

▲ The planet Venus rules in both Libra and Taurus.

YOUNG TAURUS

The child
The typical Taurus child:
- Is very quiet.
- Dislikes being the centre of attention.
- Loves nature and animals.
- Is very self-reliant.
- Tends to be introverted.
- Is usually calm and very rarely angry.
- Is extremely stubborn.
- Has physical strength and toughness.
- Likes to collect things.
- Is a steady student.

TAURUS

32

The woman

These are typical characteristics of the Taurean female, but they are by no means universal. Strong influences in an individual's birth chart, such as the positions of the planets, can distort or skew these characteristics, but they are rarely altogether absent.

Typical appearance

- Full and curvy figure.
- Luxurious hair.
- Physically strong and tough.
- Wears sensual fabrics.
- Beautiful complexion.
- Tendency to put on weight easily.
- Short limbs and broad hands and feet.

Personality

- Unshakeable moral standards.
- Takes people at face value.
- Very supportive of her friends.
- Keeps her emotions under control.
- Knows the value of everything.
- Tends to be morose.
- Very courageous.
- Ferociously protective of loved ones.

Parenting a young Taurean

Taurean children are invariably beloved by adults. They have the twin qualities of immense charm and quietness which make them seem like perfectly behaved little boys and girls. A parent who has ever tried to get a Taurean child to do something it doesn't want to do might have a different story to tell. Children may generally be stubborn, but a Taurean child is harder to move than an elephant wearing shackles. The only way to get around a sitting Bull is by appealing to its sense of morality, which is likely to be highly developed at an early age.

Young Taureans need stable surroundings. Unpredictable changes can upset them deeply, and they need to be absolutely sure that they are loved unconditionally. They will probably be fascinated by music and love harmonious patterns of colour.

▶ Your leisure

You love

- Pleasures of the flesh.
- Having plenty of cash in the bank.
- Collecting money.
- Having comfortable habits.
- Eating and drinking.

You hate

- Change for change's sake.
- Having your routine disturbed.
- Flagrant immorality.
- Being hurried.
- Having to trust people that you don't know well.

You are never happier than when you are outdoors in contact with nature. Moving fast is not your strong suit, but you can hike across mountains and through forests for days on end.

Hobbies and pastimes

Looking for a hobby? Try one of these:

- Collecting antiques or anything of high intrinsic value.
- Gentle sports or games that test stamina rather than explosive effort.
- Painting or singing.
- Growing plants.
- Theatre (preferably classics).
- Cooking or sampling exotic foods.

Your rest

There is a deep-seated streak of what some people might unkindly refer to as laziness in you. Given the chance, you would be quite happy to spend two weeks sitting around in an exclusive hotel, sampling the reassuringly expensive room service and perhaps spending an afternoon here and there being pampered in a spa. You have an actual talent for relaxing, the way that some people have a talent for doing quadratic equations in their heads: it just comes naturally.

Your ideal holiday destination would have to be in a wild and natural place, but preferably a wild and natural place with a five-star hotel.

▲ All Taureans have green fingers and find contact with nature very therapeutic.

◢ Your health

Taureans are immensely physically tough and bear pain and discomfort stoically. An unwelcome disturbance in your routine is the most likely cause of health problems.

Sickness

There are few cases in recorded history of Taureans complaining about physical discomfort. Your stubborn refusal to accept that you might be ill can lead to serious problems if it prevents you from getting the help you need.

You suffer particularly from:

- Disorders caused by over-indulgence.
- Throat infections.
- Swollen glands.
- Clinical depression.
- Constipation.

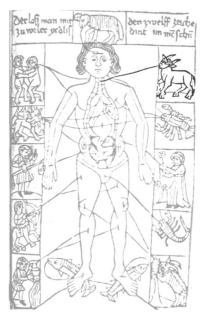

▲ A drawing from a sixteenth-century calendar shows a connection between Taurus and the human throat.

Body parts linked to Taurus

The parts of the body traditionally linked to the strong influence of Taurus are as shown on the right.

▶ An individual's birth chart will show if any of these body parts have inherited a strength or vulnerability.

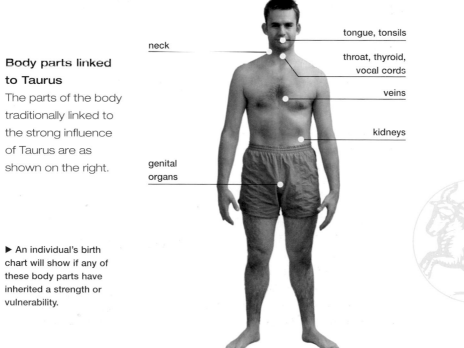

neck

tongue, tonsils

throat, thyroid, vocal cords

veins

kidneys

genital organs

▶ In love

Ruled by Venus, the goddess of love herself, you would think that your love life should proceed with serene blissfulness. Unfortunately, nobody is that lucky. Your extreme desire to possess and be stable tends to mar your relationships.

Falling in love you:
- Fall, hard, fast and, apparently, for ever.
- Plan your seduction meticulously.
- Use your masterly command of body language to send all the right signals.
- Are a little naive.

In love you expect:
- Glamour and good living.
- Absolute loyalty.
- To feel secure.
- Total honesty and high moral standards.
- To be endlessly pampered.
- Your lover to remember important dates.

How to capture a Taurean's heart
- Be extremely patient, Taureans never do anything in a rush.
- Don't try to sweep him/her off their feet with a romantic weekend away, it's bound to interfere with long-established plans.
- Make yourself appear to be as stable as you can.
- Give expensive gifts, but they must be the real thing.
- The way to a Taurean's heart is through his/her stomach.
- Don't expect passionate declarations of love; he/she could be head-over-heels about you and never say a word.

FRIENDSHIPS AT A GLANCE

Check here for personality clashes. Friendship matches are not the same as love matches. Think about it: would you actually want to marry some of your friends?

	Aries	Taurus	Gemini	Cancer	Leo	Virgo	Libra	Scorpio	Sagittarius	Capricorn	Aquarius	Pisces	Match will be
	●	●	●	●		●				●		●	friendly
					●			●			●		edgy
							●		●				trouble

TAURUS

Love matches

Extreme cases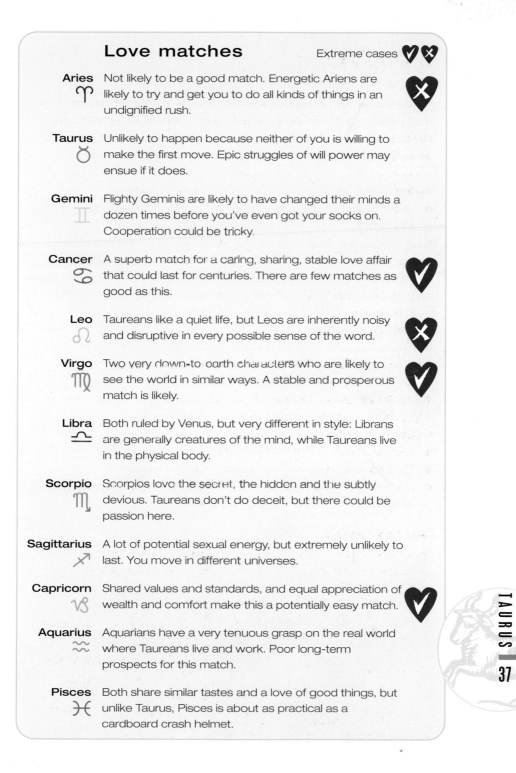

Aries ♈
Not likely to be a good match. Energetic Ariens are likely to try and get you to do all kinds of things in an undignified rush.

Taurus ♉
Unlikely to happen because neither of you is willing to make the first move. Epic struggles of will power may ensue if it does.

Gemini ♊
Flighty Geminis are likely to have changed their minds a dozen times before you've even got your socks on. Cooperation could be tricky.

Cancer ♋
A superb match for a caring, sharing, stable love affair that could last for centuries. There are few matches as good as this.

Leo ♌
Taureans like a quiet life, but Leos are inherently noisy and disruptive in every possible sense of the word.

Virgo ♍
Two very down-to-earth characters who are likely to see the world in similar ways. A stable and prosperous match is likely.

Libra ♎
Both ruled by Venus, but very different in style: Librans are generally creatures of the mind, while Taureans live in the physical body.

Scorpio ♏
Scorpios love the secret, the hidden and the subtly devious. Taureans don't do deceit, but there could be passion here.

Sagittarius ♐
A lot of potential sexual energy, but extremely unlikely to last. You move in different universes.

Capricorn ♑
Shared values and standards, and equal appreciation of wealth and comfort make this a potentially easy match.

Aquarius ♒
Aquarians have a very tenuous grasp on the real world where Taureans live and work. Poor long-term prospects for this match.

Pisces ♓
Both share similar tastes and a love of good things, but unlike Taurus, Pisces is about as practical as a cardboard crash helmet.

▶ Sex

Taureans are among the sexiest people on earth. This is surprising considering their staid image, but their sexuality runs through them as naturally as fertility in spring. Taurean women are as close to love goddesses as you can find.

Your sexuality

You are slow to show your sexual passion, but once it has been unleashed it's no more controllable than a Pacific typhoon. You are never going to be showy or openly licentious, but there are powerful currents of lustiness running deep below your calm exterior. You are instinctively in tune with your body and its needs and you are an olympic class practitioner of body language, even if you don't realize it. Taureans' taste for food and wine may be common knowledge, but those are not their only appetites.

Sexual needs:

- Pleasure for its own sake.
- A lover who can keep up with insatiable desires.
- Absolute openness; deception is the ultimate turn-off.
- Frequent and generous compliments.
- Very long, very slow bedroom interludes.

Sexual turn-ons:

- Money or expensive things.
- Food (as simple as that).
- Pleasure rather than excitement.
- Fondling and gentle nibbling.
- Sensual and secure surroundings.
- Very slow and thorough foreplay.

Love's fond Message.

Love and sex

Taureans are sometimes guilty of rather plodding logic. Just because it's true that somebody who loves you will want to have sex, it doesn't mean that somebody who wants to have sex loves you. Like all earth signs, Taurus needs security and stability to stand a chance of finding sexual bliss.

Famous Taureans

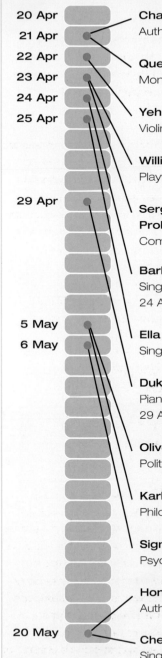

20 Apr	**Charlotte Brontë** Author, 21 April 1816
21 Apr	
22 Apr	**Queen Elizabeth II** Monarch, 21 April 1926
23 Apr	
24 Apr	**Yehudi Menuhin** Violinist, 22 April 1916
25 Apr	
	William Shakespeare Playwright, 23 April 1564
29 Apr	**Sergei Sergeyevich Prokofiev** Composer, 23 April 1891
	Barbara Streisand Singer and actress, 24 April 1942
5 May	**Ella Fitzgerald** Singer, 25 April 1915
6 May	
	Duke Ellington Pianist and composer, 29 April 1899
	Oliver Cromwell Politician, 5 May 1599
	Karl Marx Philosopher, 5 May 1818
	Sigmund Freud Psychoanalyst, 6 May 1856
	Honoré de Balzac Author, 20 May 1799
20 May	**Cher** Singer, 20 May 1946

Charlotte Brontë
(born 21 April 1816)

William Shakespeare
(born 23 April 1564)

Ella Fitzgerald
(born 25 April 1915)

Karl Marx
(born 5 May 1818)

Sigmund Freud
(born 6 May 1856)

Honoré de Balzac
(born 20 May 1799)

▶ Everyday life

A Taurean's home always feels grander and more stylish than it has any right to be. Somehow, they have the ability to make a silk purse out of a pig's ear. This is largely down to their innate sense of style and space.

Your home

One of the biggest questions that you have to consider when choosing a place to live is not 'is it close enough to the shops?' but 'is there enough room to fit all my stuff in?' Taureans are inveterate collectors. They often collect expensive objects that their built-in quality detectors enable them to amass with ease. Even if you aren't rich enough to afford shelves lined with Ming vases, you probably have some kind of collection going.

Your work

Taureans have a great capacity to see things through to the end, but they can be a bit slow in a crisis.

▲ Taureans (20 April–20 May) are born amid springtime renewal.

Job for life?

- Banking or investment.
- Interior design or landscaping.
- Family medicine.
- Farming or anything to do with caring for the land.
- Singer, actor or voice coach.
- Antique dealer or auctioneer.
- Any job where stability, reliability and a capacity for hard work are an asset.

Taurean boss

- Financially very astute.
- Usually a self-made person.
- Does nothing in haste.
- Hates flattery.
- Likes things to be done his/her way.

Taurean worker

- Very trustworthy and competent at handling money.
- Needs a regular salary and a stable environment.
- Revels in routine.
- Rarely panics.

Your appetites

Taurus is traditionally the sign of the epicure. Some, less kind, people might say the sign of the glutton. There is no doubt about it, food is one of their greatest pleasures.

You are a sensual creature, and one of the greatest sensual delights the world has to offer, in your view at least, is the very best in food and wine. Given the choice, you would eat like an emperor every night, and have a wine cellar stocked with the kind of vintages that are bought and sold in auction houses. You will try anything once, but you have a particular fondness for the exotic. A huge plate of bangers and mash with lashings of gravy is fine, but a platter of zebra steaks and Chinese artichokes would be better. Taureans are the original sweet tooths. Chocolate, in your humble opinion, is one of the finest things in creation. You probably wage constant battle against the perils of over-indulgence.

YOUR MONEY AND YOUR FORTUNE

Taureans are natural millionaires. The get-rich-quick scheme is not for you, but you are a past master at the shrewdly judged, long-term investment. To make your fortune, try these suggestions:

- Go to Hollywood and become a multi-millionaire sex symbol.
- Turn your hobby into your job.
- Charge for giving sound financial advice (and take a cut of the inevitable profits).
- Have more faith in your natural talents.
- Give full reign to your talent for collecting.
- Become a style or food guru.
- Work in a cash-based business: money multiplies magically in your hands.

gemini

the twins

21 May–20 June

Key words for Gemini, the third sign of the zodiac, are:

- Communication and persuasion
- Change and variety
- Intelligence and wit
- Curiosity and movement
- Learning and education
- Youth and freedom
- Adaptability and intuition

Your element

Gemini is the mutable air sign. You are a wind or a breeze rather than the air itself. Air can be trapped in a jar, but you can't trap a breeze in a jar any more than you can pin down a Gemini. The symbol of the twin is the key to the endlessly contradictory Geminian character. While not actually split personalities, they come close. There is a deep chasm between your mental and physical aspects.

Your character

▼ Mercury, the messenger of the gods, rules Gemini.

To others, you seem to be too restless to stand in one place, but your restlessness springs from the fact that you can't find the place you desperately want to stand in. The old adage that there are two sides to every story is laughable to a Gemini: you know there are several thousand sides. You are constantly seeking a new perspective, which is why you seem to be flitting around so much. In fact you are looking for final, solid truths. You believe in thoughts much more than feelings, which leads you to try and rationalize things that can't be rationalized, such as love and sorrow.

Your ruling planet

Gemini is ruled by Mercury, the quick-witted messenger of the gods. Mercury imparts a rapier-sharp intellect, a gift for communication, persuasiveness and the ability to be in unexpected places at unexpected times. Your verbal or communicative skills are one of your greatest assets and a tendency to revel in and spread gossip is one of your greatest weaknesses. Mercury also rules the performing arts.

Your secrets

The confidence with which Geminis can express themselves masks the deep loneliness that they often feel. Your whole life is a kind of search for something that you feel is missing. This is usually interpreted as a search for a missing twin (the twins are Gemini's astrological symbol), but it probably isn't a person at all; it's a quest to unite the deeply divided spiritual and earthly parts of your psyche. Communication is a necessity rather than a luxury for you: it's a lifeline to the rest of the world.

GEMINI

44

CHARACTERISTICS

POSITIVE

- Excellent communicator
- Inventive and original mind
- Extremely versatile
- Broad-minded
- Young at heart
- Endlessly inquisitive
- Stimulating company

NEGATIVE

- Restless and fickle
- Impractical
- Prone to depression
- Love to gossip
- Easily bored
- Unstable character
- Prone to tension and nervousness
- Superficial

LUCKY CONNECTIONS

Colour	Orange
Plants	Orchid and hybrids
Perfume	Lavender
Gemstones	Tourmaline and garnet
Metal	Quicksilver
Tarot card	The lovers
Animal	Magpie

ALONE WITH JUDY GARLAND

◀ Judy Garland (born 10 June 1922) amply demonstrated the Geminian's natural talent for performing by becoming a megastar of both stage and screen. Her drug abuse, which contributed to her early death at the age of just 47, and her serial marriages hint at strong influences from the more tortured side of the Geminian personality.

The man

These are typical characteristics of the Gemini male, but they are by no means universal. Strong influences in an individual's birth chart, such as the positions of the planets, can distort or skew these characteristics, but they are rarely altogether absent.

Typical appearance
- Taller than average.
- Rough complexion.
- High forehead.
- Hairline that recedes early.
- Quick and expressive eyes.
- Usually slim.

Personality
- Always on the move.
- Very persuasive and charming.
- Likes to socialize.
- Full of nervous energy.
- Can easily do several things at once.
- Intelligent and very well informed.
- Very witty, but superficial.
- Dresses in a striking manner.
- Rarely talks about his feelings.

▲ The planet Mercury rules in Gemini and Virgo.

YOUNG GEMINI

The child
The typical Gemini child:
- Is incredibly energetic.
- Always seems to be under your feet.
- Talks and reads at a young age.
- Has endless questions.
- Needs to explore.
- Socializes easily.
- Is an excellent mimic.
- Constantly loses things.
- Can cause chaos.
- Is very bright and precocious.

The woman

These are typical characteristics of the Gemini female, but they are by no means universal. Strong influences in an individual's birth chart, such as the positions of the planets, can distort or skew these characteristics, but they are rarely altogether absent.

Typical appearance
- Taller than average and very supple.
- Athletic muscle tone.
- Always looks younger than her age.
- Long limbs and expressive hands.
- Favours unusual clothes.
- Loves to move and dance.
- Beautiful eyes.

Personality
- Knows everything about everybody.
- Is interested in everything.
- Finds it hard to settle down.
- Is very intuitive.
- Sees good in everyone.
- Lively and fascinating conversationalist.
- Never misses a thing.
- Keeps her emotions well-hidden.

Parenting a young Gemini

Gemini kids seem to be pre-programmed to learn to talk almost before they can crawl. This is all very admirable, as long as you are not the one having to cope with the barrage of questions that seem to be their chief mode of communication. Young Gemini is inquisitiveness personified. If a parent doesn't know the answer, they are likely to go off exploring to try to find it for themselves, causing chaos in the process.

A little Gemini's mind is always active; they want to know about everything, but are hampered by a lack of patience. It's no use sitting down with charts and pictures to explain something to a Gemini; they will be six subjects further on before you've got to page two. Geminis are immensely sociable. They are likely to have dozens of friends and know things about them that you don't even know about your own mother.

▶ Your leisure

You love

- Chatting about nothing particularly important.
- Slapstick.
- Being very busy and stimulated.
- Soap operas and gossip.
- Gadgets.

You hate

- People who go on and on about the same things.
- Doing nothing.
- People finding out too much about you.

Most sports are taken far too seriously to interest you and besides, they offer far too few opportunities to talk. Social activities are your favourite form of rest and relaxation.

Hobbies and pastimes

Looking for a hobby? Try one of these:

- Learning a language (or five); you're a natural.
- Writing emails, postcards, letters to the editor, texts, graffiti, or anything.
- Getting involved in a debating society.
- Exploring and learning about something new.
- Film and video.
- Performing on stage in dance or comedy.
- Fast-paced, individual sports such as table tennis or pool.

Your rest

You don't understand 'rest' in the same way as other people. For your information, 'rest' usually means something like 'the absence of activity' or 'calm and tranquillity'.

To you, those probably sound more like definitions of boredom. It is rare to find a Gemini completely at rest; that is, doing nothing for the sake of doing nothing. Your idea of relaxation probably involves doing something that you don't have the chance to do otherwise because the rigid rules of the work-a-day world don't let you. The chance to win a good-natured argument or spend all afternoon playing with the latest electronic gadget is your ideal way of recharging your batteries. Travel also fascinates you, though you often find that it doesn't live up to your wild expectations.

▲ Geminis are naturally gifted communicators and excel in dance and performance.

Your health

Geminis are usually moving too fast to be struck by illness. Nervous exhaustion is a potential problem if you can't find a satisfactory way of relaxing and winding down.

Sickness

Geminis don't often complain, unless they are too cold or too hot, which seems to be something they just can't tolerate.

You suffer particularly from:

- Coughs and colds.
- Circulation problems.
- Exhaustion.

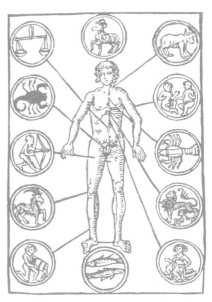

▲ A drawing from a sixteenth-century calendar shows a connection between Gemini and the arms.

Body parts linked to Gemini

The parts of the body traditionally linked to the strong influence of Gemini are as shown on the right.

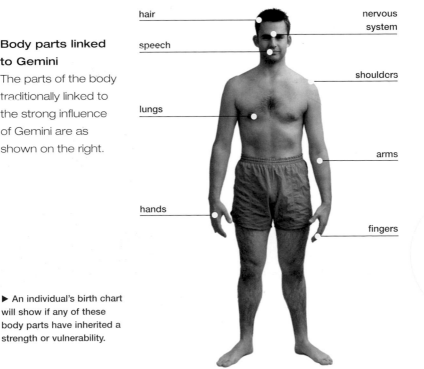

hair

speech

lungs

hands

nervous system

shoulders

arms

fingers

▶ An individual's birth chart will show if any of these body parts have inherited a strength or vulnerability.

► In love

Being in love with a Gemini is a bit like the perennial male fantasy of dating twins, except that one of the twins is the most wonderful person in the world and the other one is the Wicked Witch of the West. Not only that, but it's impossible to tell when one left the room and the other walked in.

Falling in love you:
- Are extremely confused by your emotions.
- Are very sensitive and easily hurt by unexpected reactions.
- Feel very deeply, but find it hard to express yourself.
- Appear much more unconcerned than you are.

In love you expect:
- A soul mate.
- A lover with telepathic powers.
- A very light load of emotional demands.
- To be able to get away with just about anything.
- A lover who is very patient and forgiving.

How to capture a Geminian's heart
- Never be morose or too serious about anything.
- Be ready to do or respond to anything at a moment's notice.
- Read your newspaper every day; you need to be up to date.
- Don't press him/her to talk about what they feel; Geminis rarely have a clue about what they really feel.
- Be unpredictable, but always available.
- Don't plan too far in advance.

FRIENDSHIPS AT A GLANCE

Check here for personality clashes. Friendship matches are not the same as love matches. Think about it: would you actually want to marry some of your friends?

Aries	Taurus	Gemini	Cancer	Leo	Virgo	Libra	Scorpio	Sagittarius	Capricorn	Aquarius	Pisces	Match will be
●	●	●	●	●		●				●		friendly
					●			●			●	edgy
							●		●			trouble

Love matches

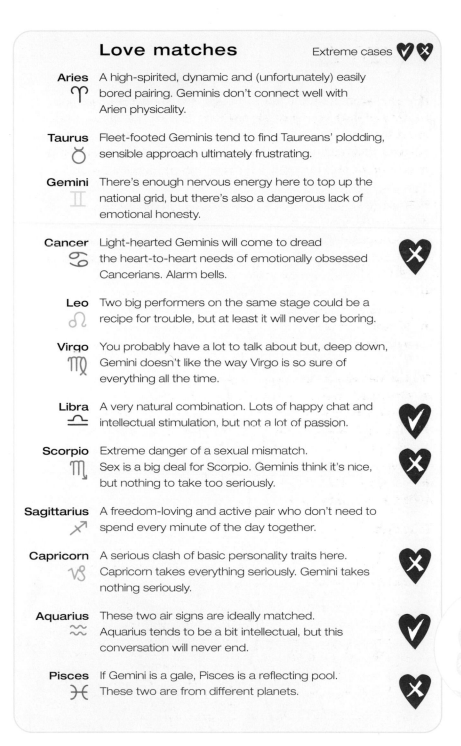

Extreme cases ♥ ✘

Aries ♈
A high-spirited, dynamic and (unfortunately) easily bored pairing. Geminis don't connect well with Arien physicality.

Taurus ♉
Fleet-footed Geminis tend to find Taureans' plodding, sensible approach ultimately frustrating.

Gemini ♊
There's enough nervous energy here to top up the national grid, but there's also a dangerous lack of emotional honesty.

Cancer ♋
Light-hearted Geminis will come to dread the heart-to-heart needs of emotionally obsessed Cancerians. Alarm bells. ✘

Leo ♌
Two big performers on the same stage could be a recipe for trouble, but at least it will never be boring.

Virgo ♍
You probably have a lot to talk about but, deep down, Gemini doesn't like the way Virgo is so sure of everything all the time.

Libra ♎
A very natural combination. Lots of happy chat and intellectual stimulation, but not a lot of passion. ♥

Scorpio ♏
Extreme danger of a sexual mismatch. Sex is a big deal for Scorpio. Geminis think it's nice, but nothing to take too seriously. ✘

Sagittarius ♐
A freedom-loving and active pair who don't need to spend every minute of the day together.

Capricorn ♑
A serious clash of basic personality traits here. Capricorn takes everything seriously. Gemini takes nothing seriously. ✘

Aquarius ♒
These two air signs are ideally matched. Aquarius tends to be a bit intellectual, but this conversation will never end. ♥

Pisces ♓
If Gemini is a gale, Pisces is a reflecting pool. These two are from different planets. ✘

GEMINI

51

▶ Sex

For you, sex is mostly in the head. You have complex and frequent fantasies. You are very matter-of-fact about the physical side of sex, a characteristic that allows you to throw yourself openly into passion without hang-ups.

Your sexuality

The Geminian reputation for promiscuity is, of course, an oversimplification. It stems from a straightforward and uninhibited approach that makes a lot of people uncomfortable. You like sex, and get more guilt-free animal pleasure from it than a lot of people, but you certainly aren't obsessed by it as the myth would have us believe. As with everything else, you tend to be rational about your pleasures, but the earthy, hidden part of your dual identity can be a lusty beast.

Sexual needs:
- A lover who can talk for hours on end.
- Experimentation, experimentation, experimentation.
- To be praised to the high heavens (even though you pretend not to care).
- Never to feel left out.

Sexual turn-ons:
- To be taken by surprise when you least expect it.
- Erotic stories and explicit, flirtation.
- To see everything that's going on (ceiling mirrors were invented by a Gemini).
- Wit and intelligence.
- Dirty talk in bed.

Love and sex

This is a very complicated one when it comes to Gemini (everything about Geminis is very complicated). Mentally, you are easily able to separate the two and act accordingly. However, there is a longing in you that this shouldn't be possible. Result: confusion. Solution: listen to your irrational instincts sometimes.

GEMINI

52

Famous Geminians

21 May

23 May
Joan Collins
Actress, 23 May 1933

24 May
Bob Dylan
Songwriter, singer,
25 May
24 May 1941

27 May
Queen Victoria
Monarch, 24 May 1819

29 May
Miles Davies
Trumpeter, 25 May 1926

Isadora Duncan
Dancer, 27 May 1878

1 Jun

Christopher Lee
3 Jun
Actor, 27 May 1922

John F Kennedy
US President, 29 May 1917

Marilyn Monroe
Actress, 1 June 1926

10 Jun
Allen Ginsberg
Poet, 3 June 1926

12 Jun
Judy Garland
Singer and actress,
10 June 1922

Anne Frank
Writer, 12 June 1929

18 Jun
Paul McCartney
Songwriter, singer,
19 Jun
18 June 1942
20 Jun

Salman Rushdie
Writer, 19 June 1947

Bob Dylan
(born 24 May 1941)

Queen Victoria
(born 24 May 1819)

Allen Ginsberg
(born 3 June 1926)

Paul McCartney
(born 18 June 1942)

Anne Frank
(born 12 June 1929)

Salman Rushdie
(born 19 June 1947)

▶ Everyday life

You give the impression that your home is not of any cosmic significance to you. This is true in the sense of what the actual place looks like, but there are things that you would find it very hard to live without.

Your home

One of the most important factors to a Gemini when choosing a home is its social context. Ideally, there should be lots of neighbours, lots of opportunities for people to pop in for a chat and, above all, lots of goings-on to gossip about. Communal living often suits Geminis, as long as it isn't taken too seriously or imposes too many rules.

Your work

Your social skills and communication skills make you an ideal coordinator and negotiator.

Job for life?
- Journalist or writer (gossip columnist springs to mind).
- Linguist or language teacher.
- Television presenter.
- Dancer or comedian.
- Any kind of work that requires communication and salesmanship.
- Electrical engineer.

▲ Geminians (21 May–20 June) are born at the time of traditional midsummer pastimes such as hawking.

Geminian boss
- Very open to new ideas.
- Communicates clearly and persuasively.
- Inspires trust and loyalty.
- Notices and queries everything.
- Hates administration.

Geminian worker
- Annoys bosses by being cleverer than they are.
- Constantly comes up with new ideas.
- Needs quick results.
- Gets things done fast.

Your appetites

It often seems as if a Gemini's mouth is far too busy talking to notice anything as mundane as food. This is, however, one of the few areas of life where you can indulge your passion for variety without a hint of emotional risk.

Geminis tend to have very peculiar eating habits. It's quite common for a Gemini to seem to become obsessed with one particular food, such as boiled eggs or peanut butter on bananas, and eat it for breakfast, lunch and dinner for months on end, only to suddenly switch to something completely different for no apparent reason. This is of course fairly characteristic of many other things that Geminis do, but it's particularly striking with food. You are probably quite happy to try just about anything that can be ingested and, at the same time, have an irrational and overwhelming aversion to one, apparently innocuous, food.

YOUR MONEY AND YOUR FORTUNE

You are a natural entrepreneur with a single fault: you find it very difficult to stick to the one thing that you are good at. Learn to do that and fame and fortune will beckon. To make your fortune, try these suggestions:

- Sell an idea for a product you really believe in (you are a natural salesperson).
- Stop embarrassing your bosses by showing how much cleverer than them you are.
- Become a political speech writer.
- Become a professional quiz competitor.
- Save money by avoiding the gadget pages in magazines.
- Put half as much effort into learning what you need to know as you do into learning other people's business.

cancer

the crab

21 June–22 July

Key words for Cancer, the fourth sign of the zodiac, are:

- Receptive sensitivity
- Home and domesticity
- Comfort and security
- Hospitality and nurture
- Wealth and philanthropy
- Dreaming and telepathy
- Family history and tradition

▶ Your element

Cancer is the cardinal water sign. Like the ocean, Cancerians are nurturing and receptive, but they can also be wildly unpredictable and emotionally stormy.

No one is more sensitive than a Cancerian; making other people happy is their greatest pleasure, and making other people unhappy is their greatest fear. You can't have a better friend than a Cancerian.

▼ The ever-constant Moon rules Cancer, and is primarily concerned with emotion.

Your character

You are able to sense the needs of others and feel that it is your responsibility to do something about them, even if the other person would prefer to be left alone. In other words, you can be a little smothering if you're not careful. You have a deep love and need for security, tradition, stability and family.

You naturally gravitate to positions of authority and responsibility, in either business or the family, and generally do very well at them. Your emotions are stormy, and other people can find the speed and ferocity with which they change bewildering.

Your ruling planet

The Moon rules Cancer. Like its phases, your moods wax and wane, although with considerably less predictability. Like the Moon, your moods are also mysterious and beyond the reach of logic. It's no coincidence that the word 'lunar' is connected with 'lunacy': there is something of the irrational in your thoughts somewhere, only occasionally expressed in your behaviour.

Your secrets

Like the crab, you are always ready to retreat at the first sign of potential hurt. Few people know how sensitive and easily hurt you are, because you don't let most people see beyond your slightly gruff, and very tough, exterior.

A lot of the time you feel as if you are walking a thin line between the insecurity of everyday life on one side, and the temptation of a complete withdrawal from the world on the other. Fortunately you will find that, as with most challenges, your tenacity and good sense will see you through, whatever life throws at you.

CANCER

58

CHARACTERISTICS

POSITIVE

- Profoundly sensitive
- Never give up
- Compassionate
- Excellent memory
- Wonderful host
- Humorous
- Great homemaker
- Deep-seated emotions
- Superbly supportive friend

NEGATIVE

- Tend to be clingy
- Hypersensitive to imagined slights
- Unpredictable moods
- Emotionally stifling
- Hold grudges forever
- Manipulative
- Introspective

LUCKY CONNECTIONS

Colours	Yellow-orange and indigo
Plants	Lotus, moonwort and almond
Perfume	Onycha
Gemstones	Pearl, amber and moonstone
Metal	Silver
Tarot card	The chariot
Animals	Crab, turtle and sphinx

First in Britain for women 20p

August 1st 1981

WOMAN'S OWN

YOUR SILVER SOUVENIR ROYAL WEDDING ISSUE

EVERY HAPPINESS TO CHARLES AND DIANA

◄ Diana, Princess of Wales (born 1 July 1961) had the typical Cancerian attributes of a caring and nurturing personality, and suffered from the typical Cancerian problems of low self-esteem and eating disorders.

CANCER

59

The man

These are typical characteristics of the Cancer male, but they are by no means universal. Strong influences in an individual's birth chart, such as the positions of the planets, can distort or skew these characteristics, but they are rarely altogether absent.

Typical appearance
- A bony physique.
- May have teeth that are unusual in some way.
- A prominent lower jaw.
- Broad shoulders.
- Plump or inclined to put on weight very easily.
- Even if slim, may appear plump.

Personality
- Very sensitive.
- Dresses conservatively.
- Dislikes conspicuous behaviour.
- Can be very cranky.
- Enjoys the limelight, but will not push himself forward.
- Is not comfortable talking about his personal life.
- Loves security and money.
- Uses roundabout tactics to get what he wants.
- Is very attached to his mother.

▲ The Moon rules in Cancer by night.

YOUNG CANCER

The child
The typical Cancer child:
- Is moody and changeable.
- Loves food, especially sweets.
- Is fascinated by colours and pictures.
- Needs lots of hugs and encouragement.
- Tends to withdraw inwardly.
- Invents invisible playmates.
- Uses tears to get what he/she wants.
- Loves to hoard things.
- Has an excellent memory.

CANCER

60

The woman

These are typical characteristics of the Cancer female, but they are by no means universal. Strong influences in an individual's birth chart, such as the positions of the planets, can distort or skew these characteristics, but they are rarely altogether absent.

Typical appearance

- Round and soft face.
- Flat-chested or very busty.
- Hips that are slimmer than her bust.
- Puts on weight easily.
- Strong bone structure.
- Long limbs compared to body size.
- Very large or very petite hands.

Personality

- Introspective and emotional.
- Prefers intuition to logic.
- Has strong maternal and caring instincts.
- Is shy, but very sexual.
- Craves material comforts and security.
- Is manipulative, but usually unconsciously.
- Has great patience and persistence.
- Is easily offended and never forgets an insult.

Parenting a young Cancerian

As children, Cancerians are fascinated by everything and are especially emotionally inquisitive. Their vivid imaginations mean that they can play alone for hours on end, but also that they have a tendency to see monsters under the bed.

Little Cancerians are rarely disobedient, because they hate to upset their parents. Discipline is easy, as long as there's plenty of warmth, approval and attention to back it up.

Share your emotions freely with them and give them lots of reassurance whenever they're afraid, which is likely to be often. Both boys and girls are likely to be keen on all kinds of sports.

▶ Your leisure

LOVES AND HATES

You love
- Anything expensive and tasteful.
- Excellent food and wine.
- Shopping therapy.
- Family and traditions.
- People who remember birthdays and turn up on time.

You hate
- Criticism, even if it's meant lightheartedly.
- Not being in control.
- People who don't appreciate your generosity.

Vigorous exercise is not something that has ever appealed to you. Social activities, charities or political causes are much more your scene when it comes to leisure time.

Hobbies and pastimes

Looking for a hobby? Try one of these:
- Mucking about in boats, sailing or swimming (but not too energetically).
- Water sports that can be played in teams.
- Gardening and any form of interior decorating.
- Looking after or breeding animals.
- Collecting antiques.
- Organizing social occasions or researching your family tree.

Your rest

You do enjoy a certain amount of lounging around, especially in luxurious and tranquil surroundings or anywhere near water. Your happiest and most relaxed times, however, are at home, surrounded by family and friends.

Warm, traditional occasions such as Christmas are your ideal, as long as everybody is either reasonably contented or willing to talk about why they aren't. At times like these you are able to allow your delicate emotional sensors free range. When you go away on holiday it must be to a kind of 'home from home' for you to be happy. A comfortably furnished cottage or an exceptionally well-appointed caravan are more your style than a windswept tent.

▲ Cancerians have a natural affinity with water. They invariably enjoy messing about in boats.

Your health

As long as you have security and plenty of affection you are as fit as a fiddle. Health problems usually arise through worry when these things are lacking.

Sickness

You tend to complain about every sniffle and sneeze, because it's a good way to get sympathy and affection from loved ones. On the other hand, serious illnesses tend to creep up on you without anyone realizing until you have sunk into a profound melancholy.

You particularly suffer from:

- Illnesses of the upper digestive tract.
- Indigestion.
- Catarrh and coughs.
- Anaemia and lowered vitality.
- Eating disorders.

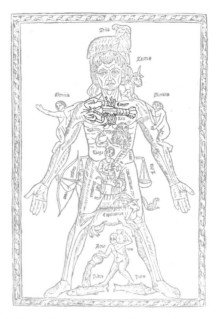

▲ A drawing from a sixteenth-century calendar shows a connection between Cancer and the human chest.

Body parts linked to Cancer

The parts of the body traditionally linked to the strong influence of Cancer are as shown in the diagram on the right.

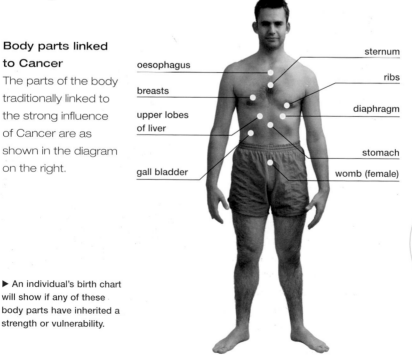

oesophagus

breasts

upper lobes of liver

gall bladder

sternum

ribs

diaphragm

stomach

womb (female)

▶ An individual's birth chart will show if any of these body parts have inherited a strength or vulnerability.

▶ In love

You have a rare talent for love of the most romantic kind. A Cancerian in love will be nurturing, intimate, responsive and devoted. You are able to ignore your lover's flaws and see only the good, even when others can't.

Falling in love you:
- Never make the first move.
- Have a pathological fear of rejection.
- Run a mile at the first sign of ridicule.
- Glow in response to honest warmth and affection.
- Become deeply attached, to the point of obsession.

In love you expect:
- Love forever.
- To have your cooking appreciated.
- To work hard for security.
- Your family always to come first.
- To be needed as the tower of strength that you are.
- Loyalty and devotion.

How to capture a Cancerian's heart
- Think roses, chocolates and candlelight.
- Think moonlight and dances.
- Ask about his/her entire family and listen to every word they say.
- Show him/her that you can cook, or take them to a relaxed homely restaurant.
- Say nice things about where he/she lives.
- Go into enormous detail about your emotions.

FRIENDSHIPS AT A GLANCE

Check here for personality clashes. Friendship matches are not the same as love matches. Think about it: would you actually want to marry some of your friends?

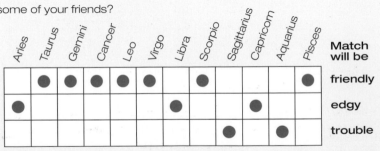

Aries	Taurus	Gemini	Cancer	Leo	Virgo	Libra	Scorpio	Sagittarius	Capricorn	Aquarius	Pisces	Match will be
	●	●	●	●	●		●				●	friendly
●						●			●			edgy
								●		●		trouble

CANCER

Love matches

Extreme cases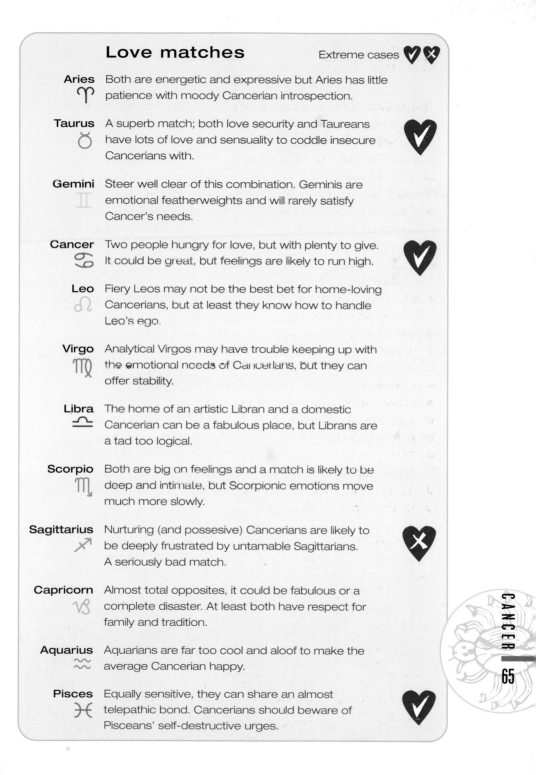

Aries ♈
Both are energetic and expressive but Aries has little patience with moody Cancerian introspection.

Taurus ♉
A superb match; both love security and Taureans have lots of love and sensuality to coddle insecure Cancerians with. ❤️

Gemini ♊
Steer well clear of this combination. Geminis are emotional featherweights and will rarely satisfy Cancer's needs.

Cancer ♋
Two people hungry for love, but with plenty to give. It could be great, but feelings are likely to run high. ❤️

Leo ♌
Fiery Leos may not be the best bet for home-loving Cancerians, but at least they know how to handle Leo's ego.

Virgo ♍
Analytical Virgos may have trouble keeping up with the emotional needs of Cancerians, but they can offer stability.

Libra ♎
The home of an artistic Libran and a domestic Cancerian can be a fabulous place, but Librans are a tad too logical.

Scorpio ♏
Both are big on feelings and a match is likely to be deep and intimate, but Scorpionic emotions move much more slowly.

Sagittarius ♐
Nurturing (and possesive) Cancerians are likely to be deeply frustrated by untamable Sagittarians. A seriously bad match. ✖️

Capricorn ♑
Almost total opposites, it could be fabulous or a complete disaster. At least both have respect for family and tradition.

Aquarius ♒
Aquarians are far too cool and aloof to make the average Cancerian happy.

Pisces ♓
Equally sensitive, they can share an almost telepathic bond. Cancerians should beware of Pisceans' self-destructive urges. ❤️

▶ Sex

Cancerians have the ability to pull off the difficult trick of appearing to be sexually innocent, yet sensual at the same time: an irresistible combination, especially in a woman.

Your sexuality

You keep your sexuality pretty much under wraps and are far too sensitive and afraid of rejection ever to be any good at outrageous flirtation. What you probably don't know is that, for all your apparent coyness, your innate lustiness leaks out all the time, and others can't help but respond to this. The way you cannot resist running your hands over lush fabrics, the way you wholeheartedly enjoy your food, and the way you laugh with unselfconscious abandon are all signs of your deep well of sexuality.

Sexual needs:

- Lots of mood making.
- To know that it's about the heart as much as the loins.
- To feel safe.
- To trust and feel completely comfortable with a lover.
- To be the centre of your lover's fantasies and to hear about them in detail.

Sexual turn-ons:

- Exotic and musky perfumes and scents.
- Rich and creamy foods.
- Running water: pools, beaches, jacuzzis and showers.
- Massages and sensual fabrics.
- Luxurious surroundings.
- Slow and lingering foreplay.
- Cuddles and pillow talk.

Love and sex

'You can't have one without the other' is one of your basic beliefs. Cancerians tend to be late developers when it comes to sex, purely because they need to be sure they have genuine feelings for a potential lover first. Teenage fumblings for the sake of curiosity are really not the Cancerian style. There must be romance first.

My VALENTINE
think of me.

Famous Cancerians

21 Jun

Jean-Paul Sartre
Philosopher, 21 June 1905

22 Jun

Prince William
Royal family, 21 June 1982

25 Jun

Meryl Streep
Actress, 22 June 1949

28 Jun

George Orwell
Writer, 25 June 1903

1 Jul

Henry VIII
Monarch, 28 June 1491

3 Jul

4 Jul

Diana, Princess of Wales
Royal family, 1 July 1961

6 Jul

Louis Armstrong
Trumpeter, singer
midnight 3/4 July 1900

Dalai Lama XIV
Spiritual leader, 6 July 1935

11 Jul

Yul Brynner
Actor, 11 July 1920

12 Jul

Bill Cosby
Comedian, 12 July 1937

15 Jul

Rembrandt van Rijn
Artist, 15 July 1606

Ernest Hemingway
Writer, 21 July 1899

Cat Stevens
Musician, 21 July 1948

21 Jul

22 Jul

Jean-Paul Sartre
(born 21 June 1905)

George Orwell
(born 25 June 1903)

Henry VIII
(born 28 June 1491)

Louis Armstrong
(born 3/4 July 1900)

Dalai Lama XIV
(born 6 July 1935)

Ernest Hemingway
(born 21 July 1899)

CANCER

67

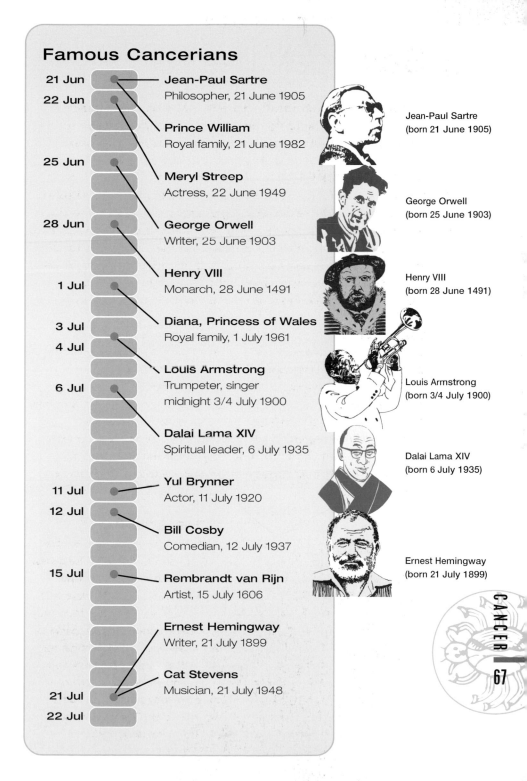

▶ Everyday life

**Home is the most important place in the world to a
Cancerian. Whether it's a penthouse bachelor pad or a
country cottage, you can always tell when you're in a
Cancerian home by the fact that you don't want to leave.**

Your home

It's impossible to overestimate the importance of the home to a
Cancerian, but that doesn't mean that you are a tedious stick-in-the-mud.
Home is a state of mind rather than a purely physical roof over your head.
Home is the sense of security and belonging that the Cancerian craves. All
Cancerians have the ability to make other people feel at home too: they
are the perfect hosts.

Your work

Bosses love Cancerian workers,
a lot of whom become bosses
themselves.

▲ Cancerians (21 June–22 July) are born
with the midsummer harvests.

Suitable jobs

- Baking, confectionery, or catering.
- Hotel or domestic work.
- Animal breeding, horticulture or
  gardening.
- Anything connected with boats,
  water, ponds, rivers, fountains,
  baths, or fishing.
- Any kind of trading, counselling,
  psychotherapy or social services.
- Nursing, or obstetrics.

Cancerian boss

- Rewards hard work.
- Never forgets anything.
- Doesn't like frivolity.
- Hard but fair.
- Dresses neatly and expects
  others to do the same.

Cancerian worker

- Motivated by money.
- Works hard and takes it
  seriously.
- Takes responsibility.
- Needs appreciation.
- Turns up every day, on time.

Your appetites

The concept of 'comfort food' was probably invented by a Cancerian. Food, like the home, is one of their main sources of security and well-being.

You would far rather sit down to a traditional Sunday roast in your own home, surrounded by family and friends, than eat exotic titbits at the world's most exclusive restaurant. This has nothing to do with being unadventurous in your tastes, in fact you probably like to try all kinds of dishes, but you almost certainly have some firm favourites that give you a warm glow of security. Instant snacks don't appeal to you at all and you probably find the very idea of fast food absurd. Unfortunately, this strong emotional connection with certain foods makes it very hard for you to follow a diet if it happens to preclude one of your favourites. You can always be relied upon to have 'just a tiny bit more' if it's offered.

YOUR MONEY AND YOUR FORTUNE

You have the ability to be ruthless in business, but are often held back by your sentimental side. Cancerians who become rich often become extremely generous philanthropists. To make your fortune, try these suggestions:

- Open a pub or restaurant and it will become an instant hit.
- Open a business on, near, or about boats and the sea.
- Go into politics and become Home Secretary.
- Start a charity and you'll soon be caring for the world.
- Learn to look the other way when you see a charity appeal, at least sometimes.
- Buy a smaller house so you can't spend so much on furniture.
- Start charging for your dinner parties, people will still come.

leo

the lion

23 July–22 August

Key words for Leo, the fifth sign of the zodiac, are:

- Pleasure and playfulness
- Creativity and recognition
- Performance and appreciation
- Generosity and loyalty
- Risk and luck
- Entertainment and hospitality
- Romance and sex appeal

INNISFIL PUBLIC LIBRARY

Your element

Leo is the fixed fire sign. Fire is the element of transmutation, of changing things from one form to another. You like to revolutionize things and turn them upside down with your boundless energy. Your sign is also fixed, which means you are prone to stubbornness and pride. On the very positive side, you are an inextinguishable source of warmth and light to your friends and family.

Your character

▼ The Sun, king of the astrological planets, rules Leo.

You love to be admired, but you only have some of the tools necessary to make it happen. Your brightness and warmth attract lots of attention, but your headstrong attitudes and inability to mask your emotions often put people's backs up, much to your surprise. You are very confident, outwardly at least, and difficult when you don't get your way, which also causes friction. You have just as much trouble hiding your positive emotions as you do your negative ones. When a happy Leo enters the room, sadness and boredom fly out the window. Your emotional and material generosity is also legendary.

Your ruling planet

The Sun, centre of the solar system, rules Leo. Like the Sun, you are a blessed source of love, light and warmth. Your connection to the Sun also gives you a creative force, as well as the power to transform destructively. Having the king of the planets (in the astrological sense) as your ruler also tends to confer a tendency to expect everyone and everything to orbit exclusively around you.

Your secrets

You crave love and respect in a way that nobody exposed to your sunny, confident exterior would guess. Winning is important to you not because it shows you are the best but because it places you at the centre of that warm glow of approval that you crave. You would be quite happy to come last if it could produce the same effect. Your generosity and unstinting cheerfulness are your way of trying to make the people around you feel better, and therefore more inclined to be warm and loving in return.

LEO

72

CHARACTERISTICS

POSITIVE

- Honest and extremely loyal
- Lively and cheerful
- Accept people for what they are
- Dignified
- Responsible
- Immensely courageous
- Unparalleled generosity
- Loving

NEGATIVE

- Headstrong
- Stubborn and wilful
- Boastful
- Attention-seeking
- Tend to take undue credit
- Seek popularity at any cost

LUCKY CONNECTIONS

Colours	Yellow and orange
Plants	Sunflower and laurel
Perfume	Olibanum
Gemstones	Catseye and chrysolite
Metal	Gold
Tarot card	Fortitude
Animals	Lion

◀ Mick Jagger (born 26 July 1943) is a textbook Leo. As an icon of rock music who has refused to step out of the limelight despite the passage of time, he clearly demonstrates the Leonine love of attention. His irrepressible energy is also a Leonine hallmark.

A TimeOut PUBLICATION. ENTERTAINMENT, THE ARTS & MUCH MORE. SEPTEMBER 1989. No.6. £1.50

20/20

JAGGER
Too old to rock'n'roll?

& JONES
Too young to die

DM10, FF30, $4.95

LIES & ANDIE MACDOWELL • THE NEW MANCHESTER BEAT • CATHERINE DENEUVE • S'EXPRESS • ... TIANANMEN SQUARE • EURYTHMICS • MEL BROOKS • MARTHA GELLHORN

The man

These are typical characteristics of the Leo male, but they are by no means universal. Strong influences in an individual's birth chart, such as the positions of the planets, can distort or skew these characteristics, but they are rarely altogether absent.

Typical appearance

- A powerful and noble bearing.
- Excellent physique.
- Dresses flamboyantly.
- Distinctive and eye-catching hair.
- Square hands and fingers.
- Narrow but intense eyes.

Personality

- Likes to show off.
- Appears to be very competent.
- Open and trusting.
- Craves excitement.
- Has many and varied friends.
- Uses charm to get what he wants.
- Generous with money and affection.
- Loves to be adored.
- Lots of sex appeal.

▲ The Sun rules in Leo by day.

YOUNG LEO

The child

The typical Leo child:

- Is rarely still.
- Talks non-stop.
- Is sunny and friendly.
- Seeks constant approval.
- Loves physical games.
- Demands lavish birthday parties.
- Is generous and sharing.
- Likes to be waited on.
- Has lots of friends.
- Steals the show.

LEO

The woman

These are typical characteristics of the Leo female, but they are by no means universal. Strong influences in an individual's birth chart, such as the positions of the planets, can distort or skew these characteristics, but they are rarely altogether absent.

Typical appearance

- Exudes dignity and class.
- Has distinctive or eye-catching hair.
- Walks with her head held high.
- Usually tall, slim and well-proportioned.
- Dresses to impress.
- Oval face.
- Looks good whatever the situation.

Personality

- Trusting and loyal.
- Lights up a room.
- Never goes unnoticed.
- Loves excitement and travel.
- Is polite and friendly to strangers.
- Loves power and wealth.
- Instinctively generous.
- Constantly, but subtly, flirtatious.

Parenting a young Leo

Young Leos are natural mischief-makers who have the ability to get away with anything by putting on a bright smile of innocence when caught. A Leo child loves to be active and, from a very early age, will exhibit the classic Leo traits of attention-seeking.

Above all young Leos are desperate to have the approval of their parents. The best means of disciplining a young Leo is not anger – which just brings out their stubborn wilfulness – but disapproval.

At school, Leo has lots of friends and is genuinely popular among his/her classmates. They love physical sports and rushing about until they are so tired that they have to be carried to bed. Freedom is essential and Leos are generally sensible enough not to abuse it.

▶ Your leisure

LOVES AND HATES

You love
- An audience.
- Being told how bright, beautiful and lucky you are.
- Buying expensive things (especially if you don't need them).
- Socializing.

You hate
- Being ignored (unlikely ever to happen).
- Dishonesty and deceit.
- Not getting your way.

King of the jungle, the lion spends a great proportion of every day asleep. Leos share this tendency to self-indulgent laziness when it's time to escape the day-to-day routine.

Hobbies and pastimes
Looking for a hobby? Try one of these:
- Sports that make you look good (skiing rather than ping pong).
- Theatrical and dramatic activities (as long as you can have the lead).
- Party games.
- Anything where you meet lots of new people all the time.
- Energetic fitness regimes.

Your rest
Nobody can be switched on all the time, not even a Leo. The brightest flame dies down eventually and even the Sun goes dark and cold for the brief, heart-stopping moment of an eclipse. Sometimes you simply need to recharge your batteries. Leos occasionally drop off the social radar screens altogether. Where are they? Uncharacteristically, either at home with their feet up watching mindless TV, or simply curled up in bed.

You love to travel for your holidays because it gives you the chance to meet and impress even more people. Even in the deepest jungle you still manage to look good.

▲ Leos love thrills and excitement, but they also like to look good. A day on the slopes couldn't be more perfect.

Your health

Overtiredness is a classic cause of illness in Leos. As is a tendency to relapse as frustration forces you to try to get back on your feet before you have fully recovered.

Sickness

The one good thing about sickness, from your point of view, is that it automatically gets you attention and sympathy. This quickly pales in comparison to the frustration of not being able to get out and about.

You suffer particularly from:

- High fevers and sudden illnesses.
- Injuries through accidents.
- Muscle problems.

Body parts linked to Leo

The parts of the body traditionally linked to the strong influence of Leo are as shown on the right.

▶ An individual's birth chart will show if any of these body parts have inherited a strength or vulnerability.

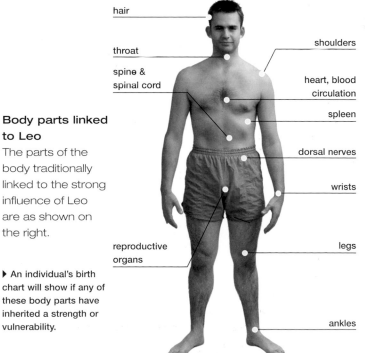

hair

throat

spine & spinal cord

shoulders

heart, blood circulation

spleen

dorsal nerves

wrists

reproductive organs

legs

ankles

▲ A drawing from a sixteenth-century calendar shows a connection between Leo and the human chest area.

▶ In love

Finding a partner can be extremely difficult for a Leo. On the one hand you want somebody who will provide you with a lifetime's supply of loyal adoration, but on the other you can't stand sycophants and are attracted to free spirits like yourself.

Falling in love you:
- Are incapable of hiding your feelings.
- Will make great sacrifices to get what you want.
- Become even more regal and noble than usual.
- Are easily disillusioned.

In love you expect:
- Loyalty and honesty that matches your own.
- To be treated like the centre of creation.
- A lover who is dependent in some ways but completely independent in others.

How to capture a Leo's heart
- Look like a million dollars and spend another million on the date.
- Remember that it is impossible to praise a Leo too much.
- Keep the gifts coming.
- Show that you can look after yourself and have some experience of the world.
- Never put him/her in a situation where they will look unstylish.
- Be absolutely honest.

FRIENDSHIPS AT A GLANCE

Check here for personality clashes. Friendship matches are not the same as love matches. Think about it: would you actually want to marry some of your friends?

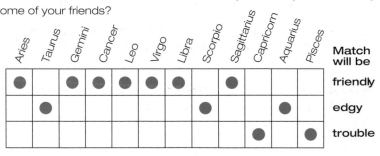

	Aries	Taurus	Gemini	Cancer	Leo	Virgo	Libra	Scorpio	Sagittarius	Capricorn	Aquarius	Pisces	Match will be
	●		●	●	●	●	●		●				friendly
		●						●			●		edgy
										●		●	trouble

Love matches

Aries
♈
Adding flame to flame is going to produce an awful lot of heat. One of the most searingly hot combinations possible.

Taurus
♉
Leo wants a rock star lifestyle. Taurus wants comfortable slippers and security. Unstoppable force meets immovable object.

Gemini
♊
Lots of fast-paced action, but there's likely to be some fierce competition for centre stage.

Cancer
♋
Not the ideal match. Fiery Leo might burn down Cancer's cosy domestic ambitions, but there's lots of emotion here.

Leo
♌
Two hungry egos under one roof means neither is going to be happy all the time, but you agree on everything else.

Virgo
♍
Virgo likes to control details, Leos wouldn't know a detail if they tripped over it. Serious cross-purposes.

Libra
♎
Librans are more even-tempered than Leos, but both love to play games. A fine and sunny forecast.

Scorpio
♏
Two drama queens on the same stage. Lots of fun, but lots of no-holds-barred battles too.

Sagittarius
♐
A pair to take the world by storm if ever there was one, as long as loyal Leo remembers Sagittarius's loner streak.

Capricorn
♑
A shared appreciation of luxury and the good things in life, but Capricorn tends to be too conservative for Leo.

Aquarius
♒
Think of this as fixed air meets fixed fire, and the surprising compatibility between these opposites becomes clear.

Pisces
♓
Leos can be enchanted by Pisces' mystical expressiveness, but Pisces doesn't respond well to Leo's pride.

▶ Sex

An extraordinary number of sex symbols down the ages have been Leos. Your sex appeal is radiantly obvious, some might even say blatant. You probably don't even realize how exceptionally alluring you can be.

Your sexuality

Your combination of naive selfishness, dynamic creativity and nerve make you an outrageously exciting sexual lure. A lot of this is purely for show, however, and problems can arise when others don't realize this.

Sexual needs:
- A lover who can cope with your need to be centre stage.
- To get whatever you want without being expected to pay it back.
- Honest desire; you are never fooled by mechanical responses.
- To be the centre of your lover's fantasies and to hear about them in detail.

Sexual turn-ons:
- Money, wealth and power.
- Glamour and fame.
- Dramatic and formal seduction or courtship.
- Adulation.
- Flirtation and playfulness.
- A lover who notices the effort you have made to look good.
- To be dominant.
- The opportunity for frequent and wild fantasies.

Love and sex

Leos are secretly very traditional and are very much in favour of the idea of marriage. The biggest problem they face in the search for love is their sky-high expectations. They expect a partner to be perfect from the first meeting and dislike the idea of having to adapt or work at getting someone else to adapt. Coupled with their innate sex-appeal this tends to produce many mismatches.

ST. VALENTINE'S Greeting.

Famous Leos

23 Jul

George Bernard Shaw
Playwright, 26 July 1856

26 Jul

Carl Jung
Psychologist, 26 July 1875

Aldous Huxley
Writer, 26 July 1894

30 Jul

Mick Jagger
Singer, 26 July 1943

Emily Brontë
Author, 30 July 1818

Alfred Hitchcock
Film director, 13 August 1899

Fidel Castro
Cuban leader, 13 August 1926

Napoleon Bonaparte
French ruler, 15 August 1769

Princess Anne
Royal family, 15 August 1950

13 Aug

Mae West
Actress, 17 August 1892

15 Aug

Robert de Niro
Actor, 17 August 1943

17 Aug

Robert Redford
Actor, 18 August 1937

18 Aug

19 Aug

Bill Clinton
US President, 19 August 1946

22 Aug

George Bernard Shaw
(born 26 July 1856)

Aldous Huxley
(born 26 July 1894)

Emily Brontë
(born 30 July 1818)

Alfred Hitchcock
(born 13 August 1899)

Fidel Castro
(born 13 August 1926)

Bill Clinton
(born 19 August 1946)

LEO

81

▶ Everyday life

Your home is the ideal arena in which to show off your good taste and, hopefully, your wealth. Leos have a knack of collecting expensive and stylish possessions whatever their actual income is.

Your home

Ideally you would live in a palatial mansion furnished with priceless antiques of impeccable style and staffed with dozens of obsequious lackeys. Unfortunately even Leos are rarely lucky enough to attract the kind of wealth that would make that kind of lifestyle possible. Nevertheless, you do everything you can to make sure your home is impressive and almost inevitably feel that it is never quite good enough.

Your work

Leos tend to rise to the top through force of character and their natural leadership abilities.

Job for life?

- Promotions and sales.
- Public relations.
- Anything in the entertainment business that puts you in the limelight.
- Travel and leisure industry.
- Politics.
- Managerial positions in almost any industry.

▲ Leonines (23 July–22 August) are born at the traditional time of the wheat harvest.

Leonine boss

- Relies on being liked for self-confidence.
- Very generous with incentives and praise.
- Tends to take the credit for everything.

Leonine worker

- Very loyal.
- Excellent at customer relations.
- Needs to have good work appreciated.
- Tends to be a bit lazy.

Your appetites

You like anything that is spicy, colourful and above all expensive. You are far from greedy, but can't resist trying something new and exotic.

Your connection with the Sun, the ruler of your sign predisposes you to have a particular affinity for citrus fruits, or indeed any kind of food that gets its colour and flavour from ripening in blazing hot sunshine. There is a definite tendency towards colourful foods in your appetites. Spicy food is also probably a favourite of yours.

You tend to have expensive tastes in foods, as with everything else, and probably have a particular outrageously-priced treat that you allow yourself on a regular basis. Fortunately, you are no glutton, so this rarely causes too much trouble for your waistline. Sometimes you choose to eat certain exotic dishes just to be seen eating them.

YOUR MONEY AND YOUR FORTUNE

You tend to spend money like water in order to keep your expensive habits up. Maddeningly for everyone else, just when it looks like you are going to go bankrupt, fortune smiles once again and piles of cash appear at your feet. To make your fortune, try these suggestions:

- Marry into money, divorce, and then marry into it again.
- Invite total strangers to lend you money.
- Become a chat-show host, stand-up comic or Hollywood star (you are easily capable).
- Start a new fashion and cash in when everyone follows.
- Move to a banana republic, start a revolution and emerge as the new president.
- Sit back and wait for the opportunity that is sure to come your way (you lucky devil).
- Sell your story to the papers.

virgo

the virgin

23 August–22 September

Key words for Virgo, the sixth sign of the zodiac, are:

Altruism and honesty

Self-improvement

Health and hygiene

Efficiency and reliability

Service and modesty

Veiled strength and sensuality

Logic and decisiveness

▶ Your element

Virgo is the mutable earth sign. Your character is like a well-ordered garden or arable landscape. Everything is in its place and cooperating to make a harmonious and productive whole. Planning, timing, balance and insight are talents that you have in abundance; just the talents a good gardener needs to get the best from the earth. You have a unique capacity to shape and mould the physical world.

Your character

▼ Mercury, the gods' messenger, rules Virgo.

You have extraordinary analytical abilities, a clear mind and an enviable capacity for concentration. As an earth sign you are patient and industrious, but you also have an idealistic and perfectionist side. Thankfully, despite all these natural gifts, you are also one of the most modest of the zodiacal characters. It's a shame that you don't value your abilities more highly; Virgoans are almost always beset by self-doubt and worry. In fact, you worry about almost everything, especially things that you have no individual capacity to influence such as global poverty or the state of the ozone layer.

Your ruling planet

Mercury, the messenger of the gods, rules Virgo. This connection gives you a superb capacity with language (although you are less of a chatterbox than Geminis, who are also ruled by Mercury), and a very sharp mind that never misses a trick. A large part of your innate modesty stems from the fact that you see yourself as an unfinished project. You may be close to perfect, but 'close' is never good enough for a Virgo.

Your secrets

You see the world through whatever the opposite of rose-tinted spectacles is. Every imperfection is glaringly obvious to you, and you find imperfections almost physically painful to behold. Unfortunately, you reserve your harshest judgement for your own character. You have a constant secret fear that you are just not good enough for your job, or your family, or your spouse. Your enthusiasm for apparently mundane tasks is a direct result of your desire to set things right.

CHARACTERISTICS

POSITIVE

- Excellent eye for detail
- Superhuman organizational abilities
- Dedicated
- Modest
- Meticulous and hardworking
- Sympathetic and supportive
- Humanitarian

NEGATIVE

- Critical
- Unable to accept relations for what they are
- Hypochondriac
- Inveterate worrier
- Overly dogmatic
- Undemonstrative
- Overdemanding

LUCKY CONNECTIONS

Colours	Yellow-green, brown, cream
Plants	Narcissus, vervain, herbs
Perfume	Narcissus
Gemstones	Peridot, opal, agate
Metal	Mercury
Tarot card	The hermit
Animals	Bat, porcupine, mink

PLAYER'S CIGARETTES

Greta Garbo

(M.G.M.)

▶ Greta Garbo (born 18 September 1905) was an actress who embodied the Virgoan traits of modesty and veiled sensuality. Her infamous reclusiveness also reflects the Virgoan characteristic of shyness.

The man

These are typical characteristics of the Virgo male, but they are by no means universal. Strong influences in an individual's birth chart, such as the positions of the planets, can distort or skew these characteristics, but they are rarely altogether absent.

Typical appearance
- Very pronounced forehead.
- Dresses carefully, with authority.
- Tall and upright.
- High hairline.
- Often has unusual feet.
- Rarely overweight.

Personality
- Practical and unsentimental.
- Loves to work hard.
- Likes to help those less fortunate.
- Very serious about responsibility.
- Subtle about his intentions.
- Notices and remembers every detail.
- Rarely relaxes.
- Can be overly critical.
- Often very good looking.

▲ The planet Mercury rules in both Virgo and Gemini.

YOUNG VIRGO

The child

The typical Virgo child:
- Is quick and alert.
- Learns with phenomenal speed.
- Is very self-critical.
- Never questions authority.
- Is self-effacing.
- Loves to imitate 'grown-up' behaviour.
- Is shy around strangers.
- Is often a fussy eater.
- Hates to be teased.
- Learns to talk and read early.

The woman

These are typical characteristics of the Virgo female, but they are by no means universal. Strong influences in an individual's birth chart, such as the positions of the planets, can distort or skew these characteristics, but they are rarely altogether absent.

Typical appearance

- Soft, beautiful eyes.
- Impeccably groomed.
- Superbly dressed.
- Rarely puts on weight.
- Well-formed mouth and lips.
- Long and pointed face.
- Perfect bust.

Personality

- Devoted to her job.
- Analytical and sharp intellect.
- Great strength of purpose.
- Loves to be of service.
- Exceptionally efficient and orderly.
- Straightforward and honest.
- Uncomfortable about expressing feelings.
- Devastatingly critical.

Parenting a young Virgo

Young Virgos are almost painfully keen to please and be seen as 'grown up'. They tend to get very upset when they get things wrong and need to be constantly reassured that it's okay to make mistakes sometimes. Virgo children often have precocious abilities thanks to their capacity for concentration and love of hard work. These should be recognized and praised as much as possible, although parents shouldn't necessarily expect these talents or interests to survive into adulthood.

Perhaps more than any other child, a young Virgo is extremely sensitive to being made fun of. Ridicule, even if it is meant in a lighthearted way, will instantly puncture their fragile self-confidence. Relationships with other children, particularly those of the opposite sex tend to be fraught with difficulties.

▶ # Your leisure

LOVES AND HATES

You love
- Improving youself.
- Being involved in details.
- Muted colours and textures.
- Being on time.
- Peace and tranquility.
- Making lists.

You hate
- Noise, crowds and confusion.
- Hypocrisy and unfairness.
- People who don't think about consequences.
- Having your schedule disrupted.

You are not a natural sportsperson, preferring intellectual and practical pursuits over pointless running around after a ball. You enjoy exercise as part of your obsessive self-improvement.

Hobbies and pastimes

Looking for a hobby? Try one of these:
- Making immensely detailed models.
- Being club secretary or organizing a league.
- Taking an Open University degree or any kind of self-improvement course.
- Theatre, concerts and plays.
- Crafts that require attention to detail.
- Books, magazines, encyclopedias and dictionaries.
- Researching history.

Your rest

'A change is as good as a rest' is a phrase that might have been coined specifically for Virgos. Yours is a sign of change and adaptation. Nothing is more restful to you than learning a new skill or finding out about a totally unfamiliar place or culture. You love to use your hands and have a talent for intricate and complex manual work.

Organization is another thing that gives you a great sense of achievement and well being (at least it would if the people you were trying to organize were not so maddeningly illogical). Sports have never held much of an attraction for you, but you enjoy them occasionally as a way of eating up your constant nervous energy.

▲ Virgoans are very good with their hands and enjoy learning new skills that can be put to practical use.

Your health

Your general good health is most at risk from your tendency to worry too much about things outside of your control. Virgos' reputation for hypochondria is not entirely unfounded.

Sickness

Sickness is particularly hard for you to cope with because it tends to mess up your carefully laid plans. You are, however, more conscientious about your health than most.

You suffer particularly from:

- Problems with the digestive system.
- Catarrh and coughs.
- Poor nutrition.

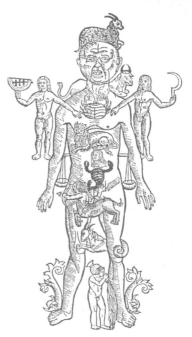

▲ A drawing from a sixteenth-century calendar shows a connection between Virgo and the digestive tract of the human body.

Body parts linked to Virgo

The parts of the body traditionally linked to the strong influence of Virgo are as shown on the right.

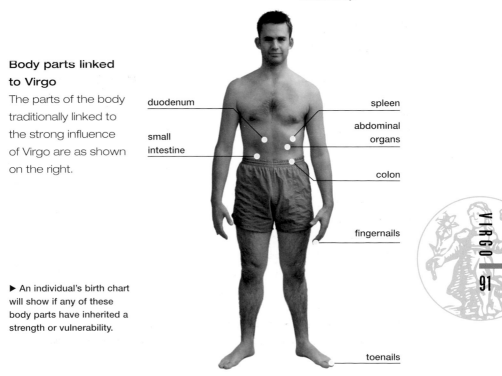

duodenum

spleen

small intestine

abdominal organs

colon

fingernails

toenails

▶ An individual's birth chart will show if any of these body parts have inherited a strength or vulnerability.

▶ In love

Finding true love is the saving grace for a Virgo (if not for all of us). It can soothe your worries and bring your numerous talents to the fore. You are a natural at love, you take great pleasure in giving as well as receiving affection.

Falling in love you:
- Love to please the object of your affections.
- Have very high standards and won't make a move until you are sure they are going to be satisfied.
- Tend to wait, wait and wait again.
- Are extremely decorous and proper.

In love you expect:
- To have a fuss made of you when you are feeling down.
- Your lover to lead a healthy lifestyle.
- Your private life to remain absolutely private.
- Not too many public displays of affection.
- Your feelings to be handled with care and sensitivity.

How to capture a Virgoan's heart
- Remember that Virgos love details, get those right and you are halfway home.
- Think health and decency.
- Never ever, under any circumstances, gossip or boast about an encounter with a Virgo; he/she will hate you forever.
- Don't be put off by a cautious response; Virgos have a secret desire to be led astray.

FRIENDSHIPS AT A GLANCE

Check here for personality clashes. Friendship matches are not the same as love matches. Think about it: would you actually want to marry some of your friends?

Aries	Taurus	Gemini	Cancer	Leo	Virgo	Libra	Scorpio	Sagittarius	Capricorn	Aquarius	Pisces	Match will be
	●		●	●	●	●	●		●			friendly
		●						●			●	edgy
●										●		trouble

Love matches

Extreme cases 🖤 ✖

Aries ♈
Aries has a tendency to leap first and look later. Virgos find that tiresome in the long run.

Taurus ♉
Two very practical, down-to-earth spirits. Taurus can teach Virgo a lot about emotions without being off-putting. 🖤

Gemini ♊
A pair that tends to make great friends but rarely great lovers. You do, however, have an infinite number of things to talk about.

Cancer ♋
A complementary match, but Cancerians' emotional outbursts tend to drive logical Virgos crazy.

Leo ♌
Virgo loves ordered detail. Leo loves flamboyant, impractical gestures. Serious clashes are inevitable. ✖

Virgo ♍
Clearly you have a lot in common and see the world in a similar way. Unfortunately two perfectionists don't always make the perfect match.

Libra ♎
A pair of thoughtful and inquiring minds that would get along great if only Libra could take everyday details a bit more seriously.

Scorpio ♏
Scorpio's inquiring mind is agile enough to keep up with Virgo and the Virgin brings out the beast in Scorpio. 🖤

Sagittarius ♐
Initial, passionate fascination is a strong likelihood, but the Archer postpones everyday details once too often.

Capricorn ♑
A natural match between two signs who share practicality, ardour and realism. Happy, stable times lie ahead. 🖤

Aquarius ♒
Virgo loves the inventive Aquarian mind, but emotionally both are all at sea. Strictly castles in the sky. ✖

Pisces ♓
Greater opposites are hard to imagine, which isn't always a bad thing. Totally unpredictable outcome.

▶ Sex

Virgoan sexuality is a minefield of complexity. Virgos appear to live up to the image of their zodiacal symbol (the Virgin), but beneath the controlled exterior there is a vast reservoir of seething sexuality just waiting to be tapped.

Your sexuality

As a lover you can be seriously electric. You have two exceptional characteristics in your favour. Firstly, you love to please, and who wouldn't appreciate a lover whose overwhelming desire is to give you as good a time as possible. Secondly, you are a master of detail. Showy dramatics are all well and good in their place, but a lover who knows the little tricks and techniques that can turn a five-minute quickie into a two-hour feature with encores is a rare and precious find.

Sexual needs:
- To be cosy and unhurried.
- To know that you are giving as much, if not more, pleasure than you are receiving.
- A lover who needs you for strong emotional reasons.
- To be given the opportunity to be a little bit wicked.

Sexual turn-ons:
- Subtlety and sophistication.
- Protracted and skilful foreplay.
- A lover who enables you to express your emotions at intimate moments.
- Sex at unusual times of the day.
- To be made to feel gorgeous.
- Domination fantasies.

Love and sex

You have a remarkably practical attitude towards the compatibility of love and sex. You see it as the ideal, but are sensible enough to realize that ideals are difficult to attain. Because you are essentially a private person, however, you will never discover the true depth of your sexuality outside of a genuinely loving relationship.

VIRGO

94

Famous Virgos

23 Aug

Leonard Bernstein
Composer, 25 August 1918

25 Aug

Sean Connery
Actor, 25 August 1930

26 Aug

Prince Albert
Royal family, 26 August 1819

27 Aug

28 Aug

29 Aug

Mother Teresa
Humanitarian,
27 August 1910

**Johann Wolfgang
von Goethe**
Writer, 28 August 1749

Michael Jackson
Singer, 29 August 1958

7 Sep

Buddy Holly
Singer, 7 September 1936

D H Lawrence
Writer, 11 September 1885

11 Sep

Agatha Christie
Writer, 15 September 1890

Louis XIV
French monarch,
16 September 1638

15 Sep

16 Sep

17 Sep

Anne Bancroft
Actress, 17 September 1931

18 Sep

19 Sep

Greta Garbo
Actress, 18 September 1905

22 Sep

Twiggy
Model, 19 September 1949

Johann Wolfgang
von Goethe
(born 28 August 1749)

Michael Jackson
(born 29 August 1958)

Buddy Holly
(born 7 September 1936)

D H Lawrence
(born 11 September 1885)

Agatha Christie
(born 15 September 1890)

Louis XIV
(born 16 September 1638)

▶ Everyday life

Virgos have a reputation for obsessive tidiness. Like all good myths this one is almost entirely untrue. A Virgo home is as likely to be messy as anyone else's, except that a Virgo will know exactly where any given thing is when it's needed.

Your home

The show-home perfection that Virgos are supposed to strive for almost certainly doesn't appeal to you at all. You are, after all, an earth sign and, as such, have a deep distrust of the clinical and overly regimented. Not only that but you couldn't possibly find the time to put everything you own carefully away in drawers and cupboards. Like other earth signs, you love to collect (even hoard) things.

Your work

Virgos tend to be the backbone of any company or commercial enterprise.

Job for life?
- Administrator.
- Civil servant (or any kind of service role).
- Skilled craftsman.
- Charity worker.
- Editor or fact-checker for the Encyclopedia Britannica.
- Dietician or health instructor.
- Police officer (or standards inspector).

▲ Virgoans (23 August–22 September) are born at the traditional time for post-harvest threshing.

Virgoan boss
- Never hesitates to express an opinion.
- Can handle complicated projects like no other.
- Hates duplicity.

Virgoan worker
- An excellent assistant.
- Does very well in service industries.
- Superb organizational abilities.
- Keen attention to detail.

Your appetites

Virgos are extremely discerning, some might even say 'fussy' when it comes to their diet. They are very conscious of the health issues connected with various foods.

The chief source of variation in your diet is your mood. You are extremely well-informed and conscientious about what you consume and would probably exist on a diet of green salads, nuts and cereals if it weren't for this one factor. There seems to be a direct connection between the mood centres of your brain and your taste buds. Although you are unlikely ever to overdose on 'unhealthy' food or alcohol, people who know you are periodically surprised to find you tucking into an 'inappropriate' treat, such as four slices of chocolate fudge cake, when the mood takes you. You must exercise care when it comes to these unpredictable cravings since you often suffer from digestive complaints.

YOUR MONEY AND YOUR FORTUNE

Your organizational abilities and swift, analytical mind should enable you to amass stacks of wealth. Unfortunately, you tend to over-analyse opportunities and let them slip from your grasp. To make your fortune, try these suggestions:

- Form a business partnership with someone far less logical than yourself (you'll drive each other mad, but make lots of money).
- Become an investigative journalist (you have a nose for when people are lying).
- Do something that everyone else thinks is far too complicated and difficult to succeed.
- Open a gym or health-food shop.
- Become a private detective and take advantage of your natural ability to uncover what has been hidden.

libra

the scales

23 September–22 October

Key words for Libra, the seventh sign of the zodiac, are:

- Diplomacy and arbitration
- Music and harmony
- Ideas and opinions
- Tact and self-control
- Refinement and sophistication
- Rationality and justice
- Charm and flirtation

▶ Your element

Libra is the cardinal air sign. Cardinal signs are rather like superheroes: they are pure representations of the qualities of the element they apply to. In your case, you are the cosmic guardian of justice and civilization. This essentially means that you strive for balance in all things, hence the symbol of the scales. Interestingly, Libra is the only zodiacal symbol that is an inanimate object.

Your character

▼ Venus, in her aspect as the Queen of Love, rules Libra.

The shorthand myth for Librans is that they are indecisive. In fact, making decisions is what you are best at. You may appear to be slow to reach conclusions, but that is just because you are considering a lot of factors that others are probably not even aware of. You are acutely aware of the weight of both the intellectual and the intuitive points of view, whereas most people disregard one in favour of the other. It is this ability to consider both sides of the equation rationally and calmly that makes you a natural diplomat and an immensely accomplished operator in social situations. Cooperation and fairness are your watchwords.

Your ruling planet

Venus rules Libra. The love goddess's influence on Libra is more social than sensual. Venus' aspects of self, beauty and love are particularly vibrant in the Libran character. You are incredibly easy to get on with and have a knack for putting people at ease. In your ideal world, universal love and peace would reign (it's no accident that it was a famous Libran named John Lennon who penned the lyrics for 'All you need is love').

Your secrets

Your love of harmony and balance are the flipside of your deep-seated fear of conflict and discord. Above all you relish harmonious social interaction because being alone is your greatest fear. This doesn't mean that you are needy for company – you are more than capable of getting along in the world under your own steam – but that you hate the idea of being disconnected from the general hussle and bustle of human society. Almost everything you do has this desire at its root.

LIBRA

100

CHARACTERISTICS

POSITIVE

- Fair-minded
- Charming
- Refined and artistic
- Even-tempered
- Sociable
- Diplomatic
- Intellectually sophisticated
- Easygoing
- Never jump to conclusions

NEGATIVE

- Fearful
- Self-indulgent
- Indecisive
- Avoid argument at any cost
- Emotionally fragile
- Manipulative
- Flirtatious

LUCKY CONNECTIONS

Colours	Green, purple, pink
Plants	Aloe, myrtle, rose
Perfume	Galbanum
Gemstone	Emerald
Metal	Copper
Tarot card	Justice
Animal	Elephant

◀ John Lennon (born 9 October 1940), told the world that 'All you need is love', a typically Libran sentiment.

LIBRA

101

The man

These are typical characteristics of the Libra male, but they are by no means universal. Strong influences in an individual's birth chart, such as the positions of the planets, can distort or skew these characteristics, but they are rarely altogether absent.

Typical appearance
- Balanced features.
- Never ugly and usually good-looking.
- Charming voice.
- Graceful and athletic build.
- Dresses with subtle discrimination.
- Often has a dimpled chin or cheeks.

Personality
- Keen to make a good impression.
- Gives wise advice freely.
- Always tries to solve conflicts.
- Likes to know all the facts.
- A master of romance.
- Likes to spend lavishly.
- Gives the impression of emotional coldness.
- Tends to be a bit vain.

▲ The planet Venus rules in both Libra and Taurus.

YOUNG LIBRA

The child
The typical Libra child:
- Is very cute and appealing as a baby.
- Doesn't like to be rushed.
- Finds it very hard to make decisions.
- Loves sweet things.
- Has immense general knowledge.
- Is very kind-hearted.
- Always plays fair.
- Hates to see parents argue.
- Is very popular at school.
- Works hard and conscientiously.

The woman

These are typical characteristics of the Libra female, but they are by no means universal. Strong influences in an individual's birth chart, such as the positions of the planets, can distort or skew these characteristics, but they are rarely altogether absent.

Typical appearance
- Slim and athletic.
- Large eyes.
- Flared nostrils.
- Large mouth and shapely lips.
- Very even teeth.
- Dresses with distinction.
- Often has dimpled cheeks.

Personality
- Very aware of her good looks.
- Uses her looks to get what she wants.
- Flirtatious but well-liked by female friends.
- Extremely diplomatic and easy going.
- Loves luxurious clothes and perfumes.
- Excellent powers of logic and analysis.
- Always tries to avoid conflicts.
- Often knows more than she reveals.

Parenting a young Libran

Young Librans are immensely skilful at persuading adults. They achieve this by combining their quick logical minds with disarming charm. Adults can find themselves bamboozled by this knockout combination to the extent that they find themselves agreeing that it is indeed logical and fair for the little Libra to stay up until 10 o'clock eating chocolate and watching television. Exaggeration aside, parents must take care not to let their young Libran talk them into spoiling them.

A harmonious environment is vital for a young Libran's development. Arguments can be deeply hurtful to little Libra, particularly if he/she is too young to understand what they are about. Socially, the young Libra is usually very well adjusted and popular. They develop their legendary diplomatic skills very early.

▶ Your leisure

LOVES AND HATES

You love
- Life's finer things.
- Convivial surroundings.
- Sharing and cooperating.
- Gentleness.
- Justice and fairness.
- Being of service.

You hate
- Arguments and discord.
- Violence and brutishness.
- People who are vacuous slaves to fashion.
- Deliberate unkindness.
- Cheap things.

Competitive sports are really too confrontational for you to enjoy them, although you probably love the conviviality of watching them. Harmony and peace are, as ever, your ideals.

Hobbies and pastimes

Looking for a hobby? Try one of these:
- Listening to or studying music (jazz bands and string quartets are your style).
- Dance (you have natural grace).
- Debating and (polite) argument.
- Eating out in romantic settings.
- Travel to romantic and sophisticated places (Shanghai rather than Machu Picchu).
- Computers and video games.

Your rest

You are exceptionally good at relaxation. Few people actually have the ability to relax properly. No doubt you pity those poor souls who spend their holidays frantically rushing around as they seek ways to 'unwind'. The idea of toasting on a beach as a bunch of fools dash around on jet skis and shriek with delight at the prospect of dangling at the end of a bungee cord fills you with horror. Proper relaxation of the kind practised by Roman emperors is almost a lost art, and Librans are the last surviving masters. Ideally, you would spend your leisure time sitting on a shaded verandah overlooking a medieval Italian city square, engaged in sophisticated conversation with a mysterious dark-haired stranger of your choice while sipping a very dry, very sophisticated martini. Now that's class!

▲ Librans generally love music, and have a natural ability with musical instruments.

Your health

Librans are generally healthy and long-lived types. It seems that peace and love are excellent promoters of good health. Isolation or constant exposure to conflict can rapidly bring on health problems.

Sickness

You are not a complainer, mainly because you don't like the idea of getting other people down. You do, however, enjoy being fussed over.

You suffer particularly from:

- Back problems.
- Kidney problems.
- Bladder infections.

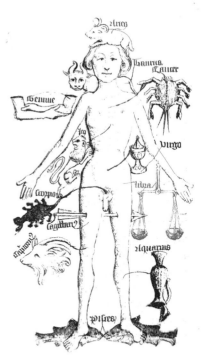

▲ A drawing from a sixteenth-century calendar shows a connection between Libra and the need for balance in the human body.

Body parts linked to Libra

The parts of the body traditionally linked to the strong influence of Libra are as shown on the right.

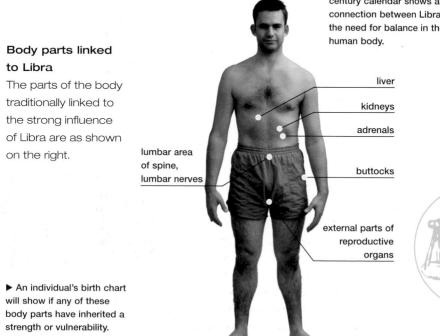

liver

kidneys

adrenals

lumbar area of spine, lumbar nerves

buttocks

external parts of reproductive organs

▶ An individual's birth chart will show if any of these body parts have inherited a strength or vulnerability.

▶ In love

Librans have the strange characteristic of believing that they are fickle and unpredictable in love, when in fact exactly the opposite is true. It may take you a little longer than others to find the right partner, but when you do it's unshakeable.

Falling in love, you:
- Ignore shortcomings (sometimes to a dangerous extent).
- Always make a subtle approach and are put off by blatant flirtation.
- Go to enormous lengths to ensure the object of your affection is never upset.

In love, you expect:
- Faithfulness and loyalty (in other words, fair play).
- To be admired (perhaps even exhalted).
- A partner who isn't overly dependent on you.
- To be amused.
- A partner who shares your refined tastes.

How to capture a Libran's heart
- Be smart, be classy, and be very good-looking.
- Never be needy.
- Take him/her to places of outstanding natural beauty (Librans respond to natural harmony).
- Tell him/her that they are the smartest, most beautiful person you have ever met (Librans are suckers for flattery).

FRIENDSHIPS AT A GLANCE

Check here for personality clashes. Friendship matches are not the same as love matches. Think about it: would you actually want to marry some of your friends?

	Aries	Taurus	Gemini	Cancer	Leo	Virgo	Libra	Scorpio	Sagittarius	Capricorn	Aquarius	Pisces	Match will be
			●		●	●	●	●	●		●		friendly
	●			●						●			edgy
		●										●	trouble

Love matches

Extreme cases ✔ ✘

Aries ♈
One of those semi-mythical 'attraction of opposites' scenarios. Very different characters that are somehow complementary.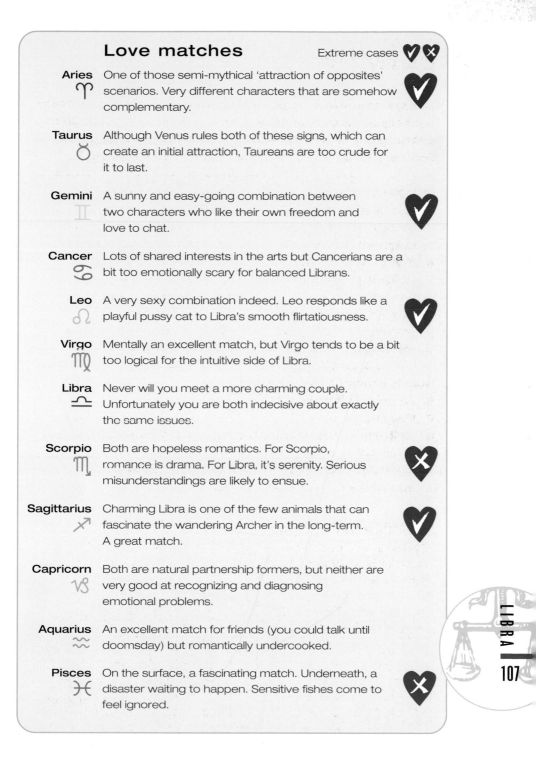

Taurus ♉
Although Venus rules both of these signs, which can create an initial attraction, Taureans are too crude for it to last.

Gemini ♊
A sunny and easy-going combination between two characters who like their own freedom and love to chat.

Cancer ♋
Lots of shared interests in the arts but Cancerians are a bit too emotionally scary for balanced Librans.

Leo ♌
A very sexy combination indeed. Leo responds like a playful pussy cat to Libra's smooth flirtatiousness.

Virgo ♍
Mentally an excellent match, but Virgo tends to be a bit too logical for the intuitive side of Libra.

Libra ♎
Never will you meet a more charming couple. Unfortunately you are both indecisive about exactly the same issues.

Scorpio ♏
Both are hopeless romantics. For Scorpio, romance is drama. For Libra, it's serenity. Serious misunderstandings are likely to ensue.

Sagittarius ♐
Charming Libra is one of the few animals that can fascinate the wandering Archer in the long-term. A great match.

Capricorn ♑
Both are natural partnership formers, but neither are very good at recognizing and diagnosing emotional problems.

Aquarius ♒
An excellent match for friends (you could talk until doomsday) but romantically undercooked.

Pisces ♓
On the surface, a fascinating match. Underneath, a disaster waiting to happen. Sensitive fishes come to feel ignored.

LIBRA

107

▶ Sex

Librans are often very good-looking, tend to have an air of sophistication and are always charming. It can come as something of a surprise to find out that under that desirable exterior they are often insecure about their sexuality.

Your sexuality

Your penchant for flirtation, and the extreme skill with which you do it, is something of a mystery, because you dislike the idea of one-night stands. You are torn by the conflicting influences of Venus, your ruling planet, which promotes free sexuality, and your abiding love of fairness and tranquility, which rule out the emotional rollercoaster of the swinging lifestyle. Quite often Librans end up at the extreme ends of the sexual spectrum, sometimes even opposite ends at different times.

Sexual needs:
- Luxurious surroundings.
- To be relaxed.
- A lover with impeccable manners.
- A lover who avoids crudity.
- A lover who is scrupulously clean and well-groomed.
- To be adored.

Sexual turn-ons:
- Extended verbal foreplay.
- Polished and sophisticated lovemaking techniques.
- Mirrors and cameras.
- Soft, almost tickling, stimulation of the skin.
- Romantic rituals.
- Fantasies of being watched.

Love and sex

Librans tend to be totally in favour of or dead set against the idea of monogamy. Either way, they tend, in practice to end up living a monogamous lifestyle because they tend to form relationships of the mind. Librans are very tempted by affairs because they think a new lover might bolster their shaky sexual confidence.

Will you be mine, Sweet Valentine.

Famous Librans

23 Sep

25 Sep — **Christopher Reeve**
Actor, 25 September 1952

26 Sep — **T S Eliot**
Poet, 26 September 1888

Julie Andrews
Actress and singer,
1 October 1935

1 Oct — **Mahatma Gandhi**
Religious and social leader,
2 Oct — 2 October 1869

4 Oct — **Groucho Marx**
5 Oct — Comedian, 2 October 1890
6 Oct

Charlton Heston
Actor, 4 October 1923

Bob Geldof
9 Oct — Musician, fundraiser,
5 October 1954

Le Corbusier
Architect, 6 October 1887

13 Oct — **John Lennon**
Musician, songwriter,
15 Oct — 9 October 1940

Margaret Thatcher
18 Oct — Politician,
13 October 1925

Oscar Wilde
Writer, 15 October 1856

22 Oct — **Martina Navratilova**
Tennis player,
18 October 1956

T S Eliot
(born 26 September
1888)

Mahatma Gandhi
(born 2 October 1869)

Groucho Marx
(born 2 October 1890)

Bob Geldof
(born 5 October 1954)

Margaret Thatcher
(born 13 October 1925)

Oscar Wilde
(born 15 October 1856)

LIBRA

109

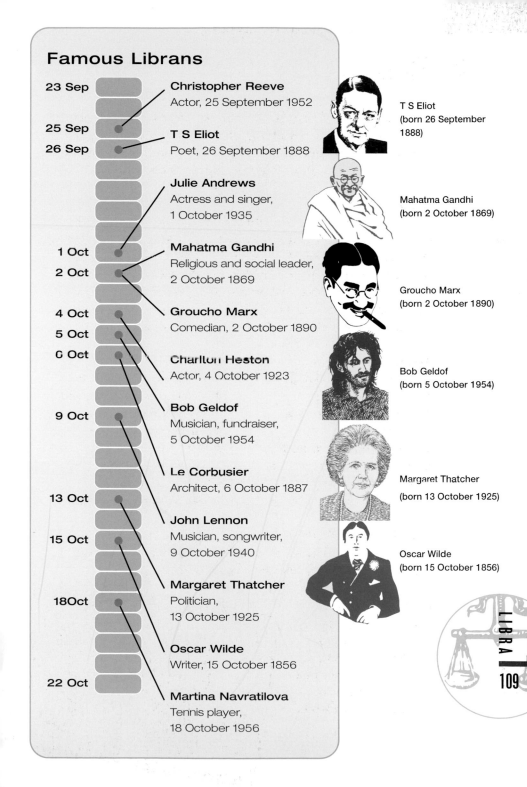

▶ Everyday life

The home of a Libran is invariably a comfortable and friendly place. Librans' twin talents of relaxation and sociability are often most clearly expressed in the way they set up home.

Your home

You have discriminating tastes which almost certainly show through in your home. Your possessions don't have to be expensive, but they do have to be in the best possible taste. Librans are great art lovers, so you can expect plenty of visual interest and a top-of-the-range stereo system. Understatement is another defining feature of Libran taste, so don't expect things to be too sumptuous in a Libran home. Above all, the Libran's home is a place of harmony where house guests are treasured.

Your work

Librans hate being ordered about, so they usually aspire to be in charge, or to run their own business.

Job for life?

- Legal professions (you have an innate sense of justice).
- Diplomacy, but not politics (you are too good at seeing other people's points of view).
- Civil rights campaigner.
- Fashion designer or artist.
- Handling or manipulating money.
- Any kind of partnership.

▲ Librans (23 September–22 October) are born at the traditional time of grape harvests.

Libran boss

- Considers all opinions before reaching a decision.
- Creates a restful, unhurried working environment.
- Is very good with money.
- Analyses rationally.

Libran worker

- Always honest.
- Needs regular rest and relaxation.
- Excellent mediator.
- Likes the idea of unions and cooperatives.

LIBRA

Your appetites

In a restaurant you are far more likely to be checking out the decor than the menu. At least, that is, until the sweet trolley arrives, at which point your attention becomes rigid.

Venus, your ruling planet, gives you a taste for the voluptuous. Fruits are a particular favourite of yours. At least they are healthy, which is more than can be said for the cream- and butter-laden dishes that usually take your fancy. You like the look of food almost as much as you like the taste, and you especially like the look of food if it appears to contain more calories than the entire chocolate output of Belgium. Your weakness for fads is very pronounced in this area. You just have to have the latest cookbook from the TV chef of the moment, even though you don't really like cooking. Inevitably, you face an almost constant battle with your weight, and are prone to trying out faddish diets.

YOUR MONEY AND YOUR FORTUNE

You have a talent for handling and investing money and probably have a reputation for trustworthiness. Your overwhelming desire to be in charge can make you resent working for others, but you need to be patient and wait until the time is right for striking out on your own. To make your fortune, try these suggestions:

- Charm someone into giving you a large sum of money to start up your own business.
- Put a pound in a jar every time you change your mind.
- Stop trying to right the world's wrongs, or at least think of a way of making it pay.
- Form a partnership with someone much less logical and cautious; they will drive you mad, but you will probably make a fortune together.
- Become a model and gain instant sex-symbol status.
- Find a way of profiting from your natural good taste.

scorpio

the scorpion

23 October–21 November

Key words for Scorpio, the eighth sign of the zodiac, are:

- Death, sex and money
- Passion and discovery
- Transformation and metamorphosis
- Investments and inheritance
- Secrets, magic and taboos
- Honesty and revolution
- Privacy and the unconscious

▶ Your element

Scorpio is the fixed water sign. This might be surprising if you are familiar with the myth that Scorpios are fiery and passionate (and who hasn't heard it?). However, the old adage that 'still waters run deep' is far more symbolic of the Scorpionic character. Like a broad meandering river, Scorpios are relentless and eventually wear down any and all opposition.

Your character

▼ Pluto, the symbol of extremes, rules Scorpio with Mars.

Scorpios have had such a bad press down the ages that many born under this sign are afraid to admit it. Obsessiveness, vengefulness, jealousy and spite are all supposed to be Scorpionic characteristics. Part of the reason Scorpios are afraid to admit to their zodiacal description is because they know it to be partly true. There is no doubt that your passions run deep, and not a few of them are dark. Truth is the key here. A Scorpio is no more capable of ignoring the truth, however unpleasant, than a fish is of not noticing water. You live and feel life to the full, even the darker areas that others try not to acknowledge.

Your ruling planet

Pluto, ancient god of the underworld, rules Scorpio. Pluto is a symbol of extremes. It is, after all, the most remote and least understood planet in the solar system. Pluto also represents transformations and confers on you the power to turn the world upside down. World inverting is something you probably do on a daily basis, especially when you make those cuttingly truthful remarks that smash through taboos as if they didn't exist.

Your secrets

Scorpios are far from dumb, which is why they are fully aware of the fact that their honesty can be controversial at times. For this reason, you tend to be tremendously secretive. This is often misinterpreted as sneakiness or cunning. On the other hand, if you let loose and tell people what you really think, you are accused of spitefulness or insensitivity. You really can't win either way. Having a more direct line to the unvarnished truth than most people is a burden you will always have to cope with.

SCORPIO

114

CHARACTERISTICS

POSITIVE

- Penetrating intellect
- Magnetic personality
- Completely unshockable
- Understand shortcomings
- Dynamic and tenacious
- Self-critical
- Sensual

NEGATIVE

- Self-destructive tendencies
- Obstinate
- Quick-tempered
- Suspicious
- Extremely moody
- Jealous
- Possessive
- Insensitive

LUCKY CONNECTIONS

Colours	Deep red, blue-green
Plants	Cactus, ivy, oak
Perfume	Siamese benzoin
Gemstones	Turquoise, snakestone, ruby
Metals	Iron, steel
Tarot card	Death (regeneration)
Animals	Wolf, grey lizard

success and failure of
picasso

◀ Pablo Picasso (born 25 October 1881) revolutionized the visual arts in a way that only a Scorpio, with their talent for transformation, could. His magnetic personality, another Scorpionic characteristic, contributed to his lasting fame.

The man

These are typical characteristics of the Scorpio male, but they are by no means universal. Strong influences in an individual's birth chart, such as the positions of the planets, can distort or skew these characteristics, but they are rarely altogether absent.

Typical appearance

- Strong and distinctive features.
- Penetrating gaze.
- Unusually hairy body.
- Athletic build and rarely gains weight.
- Tends to become bald at an early age.
- Disproportionately short limbs.

Personality

- Never self-effacing.
- Conspicuously possessive.
- Gives absolutely honest advice.
- Very self-controlled.
- Has an air of danger and mystery.
- Might be a saint or a sinner.
- Pursues his interests passionately.
- Very courageous, physically and mentally.
- Never forgets a favour, or an insult.

▲ The planet Mars rules in both Scorpio and Aries.

YOUNG SCORPIO

The child

The typical Scorpio child:

- Is secretive.
- Is highly suspicious of strangers.
- Has a terrible temper.
- Is very inquisitive.
- Has understanding beyond his/her years.
- Can be spiteful.
- Respects strength.
- Takes advantage of weakness.
- Is disarmingly honest.
- Has very clear desires.

SCORPIO

116

The woman

These are typical characteristics of the Scorpio female, but they are by no means universal. Strong influences in an individual's birth chart, such as the positions of the planets, can distort or skew these characteristics, but they are rarely altogether absent.

Typical appearance

- Compact body.
- Often shorter than average.
- Tends to have short legs.
- Magnetic looks.
- Penetrating eyes.
- Very mobile facial expressions.
- Wide and shapely hips.

Personality

- Only smiles or frowns when she means it.
- Tends to try to dominate.
- Is fiercely loyal to family and home.
- Has very strict personal standards.
- Craves freedom.
- Can be devastatingly vindictive.
- Almost never flirts or flatters.
- Never forgets a favour, or an insult.

Parenting a young Scorpio

Like a lot of kids, young Scorpios are intensely inquisitive. Unlike other kids they have an instinctive feel for when their curiosity has led them into an area that adults feel uncomfortable talking about, but this only makes their curiosity stronger. Parents of a Scorpio can find themselves constantly being ambushed by questions of a shockingly frank nature. These are by no means restricted to sex. Death, disease and other taboo subjects also fascinate young Scorpio. This tends to give the impression of an unhealthy obsession. In fact it is just a symptom of Scorpio's craving for the truth. It is the fact that they can tell they are not being told the whole truth that interests them, not the sordid details. The flip side of this coin is the way that Scorpio children love secrecy. They love to have a private place that nobody knows about, or a secret box that can be locked with a key.

▶ Your leisure

You love

- The truth (at any cost).
- Discovering hidden causes and motivations.
- Being where the action is.
- Sex (it's a cliche, but that doesn't make it untrue).

You hate

- Having your character or motivations analysed.
- Having to trust a stranger.
- Insincere flattery.
- Shallowness.

Your vigourously physical side enjoys sports, but it is the tactics rather than the sweat that really get you going. You also enjoy taking things (or people) apart to see what makes them tick.

Hobbies and pastimes

Looking for a hobby? Try one of these:

- Tactical sports or games.
- Science (probing the mysteries of the universe).
- Detective fiction and treasure hunting (amateur archaeology, for example).
- Confrontational debating (perhaps local politics).
- Dabble in the stock market (if anyone can figure out how it works, it's you).

Your rest

You don't really do relaxation. Scorpios have been known to go to extraordinary lengths to avoid going on holiday or taking time off. It's not unknown for Scorpios to suffer sudden injuries or mysterious illnesses that prevent them from taking that two-week beach holiday, only to miraculously recover once the plane has safely left.

This endless drive can be very damaging to your mental and physical wellbeing, which is why it is vitally important that you develop an interest outside of your day-to-day work. Since truth and investigation are your greatest passions, a hobby that allows you to take things apart and investigate their inner workings is the ideal.

▲ Scorpios enjoy physical sports, particularly those that involve some tactical thinking.

Your health

Overwork and the zealous pursuit of goals are the greatest threats to your health. You generally have excellent health and have a phoenix-like ability to recover from serious illness.

Sickness

Accidents and injuries are a common problem for Scorpios, you really should stop pushing yourself so hard. In keeping with the Scorpionic theme of mystery, inexplicable sicknesses are also common.

You suffer particularly from:
- Nose and throat problems.
- Hernias and piles.
- Problems with reproductive organs,

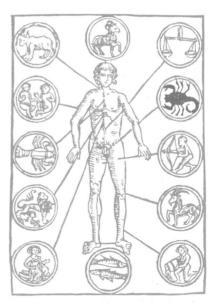

▲ A sixteenth-century calendar shows the connection between Scorpio and the reproductive organs.

Body parts linked to Scorpio

The parts of the body traditionally linked to the strong influence of Scorpio are as shown on the right.

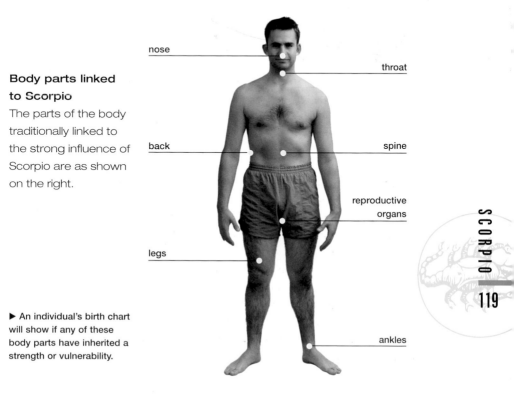

nose

throat

back

spine

reproductive organs

legs

ankles

▶ An individual's birth chart will show if any of these body parts have inherited a strength or vulnerability.

In love

Perhaps surprisingly, considering their acerbic exteriors, Scorpios have hearts made of glass. Almost every Scorpio has had his or her heart catastrophically broken, usually when very young, and they struggle to cope with this.

Falling in love you:
- Are extremely secretive about your attraction.
- Rarely display affection (which can make the whole business very difficult).
- Are sometimes much too frank (try not to be so intense all the time, it's a bit frightening).

In love you expect:
- To be able to keep some things secret.
- Absolute fidelity (old wounds heal very slowly).
- An extremely forgiving lover.
- A lover who appreciates how lucky they are to be given access to your inner thoughts.

How to capture a Scorpion's heart
- Be secretive, suggestive and a little bit aggressive (remember, it's impossible to shock a Scorpion).
- Be romantic, but never shallow (think Bogart in the rain, not heart-shaped helium balloons).
- Let him/her know how fascinating you think they are (Scorpio will be the first to agree with you).
- Don't expect to be let in easily.

FRIENDSHIPS AT A GLANCE

Check here for personality clashes. Friendship matches are not the same as love matches. Think about it: would you actually want to marry some of your friends?

Aries	Taurus	Gemini	Cancer	Leo	Virgo	Libra	Scorpio	Sagittarius	Capricorn	Aquarius	Pisces	Match will be
			●	●	●	●	●	●			●	friendly
	●		●							●		edgy
●		●										trouble

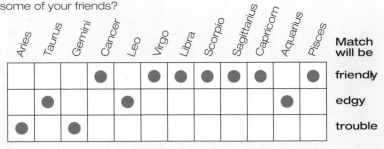

Love matches

Extreme cases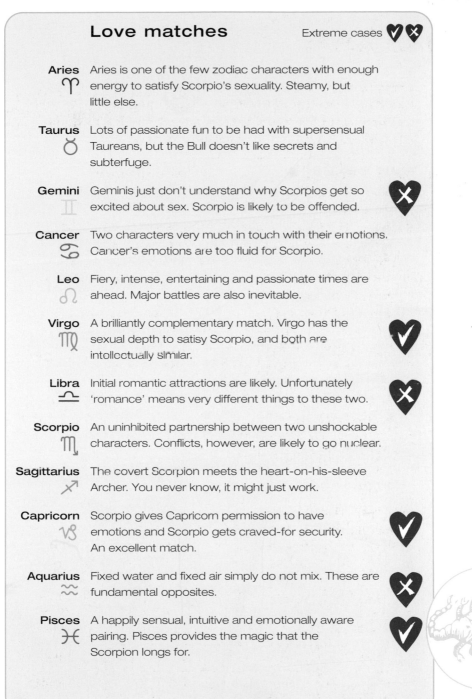

Aries
♈
Aries is one of the few zodiac characters with enough energy to satisfy Scorpio's sexuality. Steamy, but little else.

Taurus
♉
Lots of passionate fun to be had with supersensual Taureans, but the Bull doesn't like secrets and subterfuge.

Gemini
♊
Geminis just don't understand why Scorpios get so excited about sex. Scorpio is likely to be offended.

Cancer
♋
Two characters very much in touch with their emotions. Cancer's emotions are too fluid for Scorpio.

Leo
♌
Fiery, intense, entertaining and passionate times are ahead. Major battles are also inevitable.

Virgo
♍
A brilliantly complementary match. Virgo has the sexual depth to satisy Scorpio, and both are intollectually similar.

Libra
♎
Initial romantic attractions are likely. Unfortunately 'romance' means very different things to these two.

Scorpio
♏
An uninhibited partnership between two unshockable characters. Conflicts, however, are likely to go nuclear.

Sagittarius
♐
The covert Scorpion meets the heart-on-his-sleeve Archer. You never know, it might just work.

Capricorn
♑
Scorpio gives Capricorn permission to have emotions and Scorpio gets craved-for security. An excellent match.

Aquarius
♒
Fixed water and fixed air simply do not mix. These are fundamental opposites.

Pisces
♓
A happily sensual, intuitive and emotionally aware pairing. Pisces provides the magic that the Scorpion longs for.

▶ Sex

Scorpios are fascinated by sex. For them it is the central mystery of a world full of mysteries. This doesn't necessarily mean that Scorpios have to have sex. A Scorpio might be a fanatical celibate as much as a porn star.

Your sexuality

The myth of the sexually potent scorpion, which seems to be almost universally known, can be a difficult one to live up to. Even mentioning that you are a Scorpio can have potential partners diving for cover under the misapprehension that you will expect them to be a sexual superman or woman with an encyclopaedic knowledge of the *Karma Sutra*. Your fascination is not so much with the act itself, but with the way that it tangles head and heart and body into a dense and complex mystery.

Sexual needs:
- Variety (you are an inveterate sexual experimenter).
- Good, honest lust (you need a partner who isn't afraid of his/her sexuality).
- To be in control (sex and power are inseparable for you).
- A lover with stamina (quickies are not your scene).

Sexual turn-ons:
- Sex in exotic or unusual places.
- Masochistic and domination fantasies.
- Erotic stories and films.
- Any competitive activity.
- A lover with unusual or unconventional looks.
- Uncovering a lover's sexual hang-ups.

Love and sex

Oddly enough, given Scorpio's rapacious sexual reputation, you can't really conceive of sex without love. This is largely because you tend to see love as a part of sex, rather than the other way around. It is all part of the mystery for you. Why does the simple act of sex provoke such strong emotions, you wonder.

Love and sunshine dwell with thee

Famous Scorpios

23 Oct		**Pablo Picasso** Artist, 25 October 1881
25 Oct		**Dylan Thomas** Poet, 27 October 1914
27 Oct		**Sylvia Plath** Poet, 27 October 1932
		Art Garfunkel Musician, 5 November 1941
		Marie Curie Chemist, 7 November 1867
		Aleksandr Porfiryevich Borodin Composer, 12 November 1833
5 Nov		**Robert Louis Stevenson** Author, 13 November 1850
7 Nov		**Jawaharial Nehru** Indian Politician, 14 November 1889
12 Nov		**Prince Charles** Heir to throne, 14 November 1948
13 Nov		
14 Nov		
15 Nov		**Petula Clark** Singer, 15 November 1932
19 Nov		**Martin Luther** Theologian, 19 November 1483
21 Nov		**Indira Gandhi** Indian politician, 19 November 1917

Dylan Thomas
(born 27 October 1914)

Sylvia Plath
(born 27 October 1932)

Marie Curie
(born 7 November 1867)

Jawaharial Nehru
(born 14 November 1889)

Martin Luther
(born 19 November 1483)

Indira Gandhi
(born 19 November 1917)

▶ Everyday life

'A Scorpio's home is his castle' is how the adage should read. That childhood love of secret hiding places and private bolt holes carries over into an adult obsession with territorial privacy.

Your home

The classic Scorpio has so many locks on his doors, high fences and burglar alarms that it inevitably leads neighbours to wonder what you are hiding behind your tightly closed doors. It's just another manifestation of your character that tends to make people suspicious. The truth is that your home is the one place where you can afford to let down your guard.

Your work

Scorpios are tireless and effective leaders, but they can also be a little scary at times.

Job for life?

- MI6 agent or senior detective.
- Pathologist or surgeon.
- Stockbroker or market analyst.
- Any job that allows you to take things apart and see how they tick (mechanic, scientist, researcher).
- Psychologist or psychiatrist (painful and repressed truths are your speciality).

▲ Scorpions (23 October–21 November) are born at the traditional time of sowing the land.

Scorpionic boss
- Can solve apparently impossible problems.
- Very motivating.
- Competitive, but keeps it hidden.

Scorpionic worker
- Never accepts defeat.
- Hardly ever takes time off.
- Career-minded.
- Is sometimes too honest to be popular.

Your appetites

Scorpios don't have any overwhelmingly strong connections with food or drink. Perhaps food just isn't mysterious or peculiar enough to interest them particularly.

Your taste in food, insofar as you have any particular tastes, tends towards the spicy and the strongly flavoured. Basil, cinnamon, curry, garlic and ginger are probably prominent in your kitchen. If there is any food that excites Scorpios it is garlic. You tend to regard garlic not as a subtle flavouring, but as a vegetable to be eaten whole and unadulterated (possibly even raw). You also have a preference, though a vague one, to food that has a deep red colour. Over-indulgence in those hot sauces that you like can lead to obvious digestive problems. Alcohol is also something you need to be wary of; it tends to make you a bit more honest than is really appropriate.

YOUR MONEY AND YOUR FORTUNE

Your talent for making money is only matched by your talent for spending it. You have the toughness, cunning and confidence to make it big in business, and money can buy you the privacy and security that you crave. To make your fortune, try these suggestions:

● Apply the same discipline to your finances that you do to everything else.
● Pretend all your money actually belongs to someone else and act accordingly.
● Get into industrial espionage.
● Start a sex clinic.
● Do something incredibly risky with every penny riding on it (nobody has more steely nerves than you).
● Do seven impossible things before breakfast.

sagittarius

the archer

22 November–21 December

Key words for Sagittarius, the ninth sign of the zodiac, are:

- Philosophy and religion
- Optimism and positivity
- Travel and freedom
- Generosity and honesty
- Wit and intuition
- Justice and idealism
- Animals and nature

▶ Your element

Sagittarius is the mutable fire sign. You are closer in character to a wildly unpredictable bushfire started by a lightning strike than a gentle, toe-warming hearth. The fire side of your character gives you warmth and optimism while your mutability gives you the power to transform situations (hopefully for the better). You share with fire both a joyfulness and a stunning lack of subtlety.

▼ Jupiter, the lord of luck and opportunity, rules Sagittarius.

Your character

You are one of those happy souls who approaches life as an adventure. Good humour, philosophy, optimism and a plentiful supply of biscuits can get you through anything. You not only want to see the world (Sagittarius is traditionally the sign of travel), you also want to understand it and its people. Despite your philosophical bent, which is born from your sense of wonder, you are far from a stuffy academic. You are a natural comedian and lover. Luck always seems to be on your side, although this is actually an illusion created by your ability to take setbacks in your stride and your knack of constantly emphasizing the positive.

Your ruling planet

Jupiter, the Roman king of the gods, rules Sagittarius. The word 'jovial' comes directly from the Latin for Jupiter and is the term that best describes your character. Jupiter is also the lord of luck and opportunity. Abundance, learning, optimism and the kind of good cheer associated with foaming mugs of ale are also conferred by the touch of Jupiter. On the negative side, excesses of all kinds are attributed to the planet.

Your secrets

Sagittarians are said to fear rules, restrictions and bureaucracy, and it is certainly true that you hate to be held back, but your real fears run a little deeper than that. What you secretly dread is the idea that pain is, in some sense, a necessary part of life. Your dislike of rules really springs from your horror at the realization that rules are sometimes necessary. Deep down, you know this is true, but you don't really want to believe it. You care deeply about your fellow human beings and curse the fact that they suffer.

SAGITTARIUS

CHARACTERISTICS
POSITIVE

- Boundless optimism
- Very open to spiritual ideas
- Always see the best in people
- Incapable of holding a grudge
- Honest and fair
- Inquiring mind
- Profoundly humanitarian

NEGATIVE

- Hot-headed
- Self-indulgent
- Quick to judge
- Excessively blunt
- Impatient
- Manipulative
- Poor planner
- Refuse to acknowledge negative feelings

LUCKY CONNECTIONS

Colours	Blue, royal blue, purple, white
Plants	Rush, oak, fig, hyssop
Perfume	Lignaloes
Gemstones	Jacinth, lapis lazuli
Metal	Tin
Tarot card	Temperance
Animals	Horse, dog

◀ Winston Churchill (born 30 November 1874) was overlooked as a politician until the moment of national crisis came, when he emerged as a leader and potent symbol of hope and fortitude – exactly what you would expect from a Sagittarian.

ELD., MIDDX.

Churchill Centenary 5½p

SAGITTARIUS

The man

These are typical characteristics of the Sagittarius male, but they are by no means universal. Strong influences in an individual's birth chart, such as the positions of the planets, can distort or skew these characteristics, but they are rarely altogether absent.

Typical appearance
- An excellent physique.
- Exceptionally thick and luxuriant hair.
- Highly distinctive features.
- Looks younger than his years.
- Moves and walks confidently.
- Tends to dress unconventionally.

Personality
- Inveterate risk-taker.
- Enjoys physical danger.
- Humorous and outgoing.
- Forgetful and clumsy.
- Trusting to the point of childishness.
- Never deliberately cruel.
- Painfully tactless.
- Loves to learn and create.
- Laughs easily.

▲ The planet Jupiter rules in both Sagittarius and Pisces.

YOUNG SAGITTARIUS

The child
The typical Sagittarian child:
- Is happy and playful.
- Expects to be loved by everyone.
- Loves to meet new people.
- Acts on impulse.
- Adores animals.
- Tends to get a lot of scrapes and bruises.
- Is extremely trusting.
- Endlessly asks 'why?'
- Never sits still.
- Hates to be alone.

SAGITTARIUS

130

The woman

These are typical characteristics of the Sagittarius female, but they are by no means universal. Strong influences in an individual's birth chart, such as the positions of the planets, can distort or skew these characteristics, but they are rarely altogether absent.

Typical appearance
- Oval face and a high forehead.
- Moves with grace and purpose.
- Tends to be slim and tall.
- Bright and honest eyes.
- Thick and luxuriant hair.
- Looks younger than her years.
- Has a 'unique' dress sense.

Personality
- Laughs at her own misfortunes.
- Quick-tempered, but easily placated.
- Extremely kind-hearted and caring.
- Tends to preach.
- Has unshakeable moral standards.
- Has strong spiritual beliefs.
- Believes in equality.
- Painfully tactless.

Parenting a young Sagittarian
Honesty is not just the best policy for the parent of a young Sagittarius, it's the only available option. The question 'why?' was clearly invented by a Sagittarian, and probably one that had only just learned to speak. Young Sagittarius can spot dishonesty a mile off, and is quick to learn the power of sarcasm for poking fun at adult double standards.

Young archers don't respond well to rules and regulations, especially if they don't understand them. On the other hand, they tend to have well-formed and strict codes of self-conduct, so they can be trusted to behave well, if not exactly within the rules. This dislike of boundaries definitely extends to social situations and a young Sagittarian will quite happily strike up a bright and cheerful conversation with a total stranger. This a quality that tends to make them well-liked among their peers.

▶ Your leisure

LOVES AND HATES

You love

- Happy people and situations.
- An abundance of good food and wine.
- Spiritualism and hope.
- Getting to the bottom of mysteries.
- Travel and freedom.

You hate

- Unhappiness and sombre occasions.
- Pessimism and resignation.
- Too much attention to surface details.

You generally enjoy vigorous and dangerous team sports such as rugby or hockey. The social aspects of sport are as important to you as the play, and much more important than winning.

Hobbies and pastimes

Looking for a hobby? Try one of these:

- Travel and exploration in strange and mysterious places.
- Learning languages and investigating foreign cultures.
- Solving problems.
- Food and drink.
- Gambling and games of chance (beware of your tendency to excess).
- Caring for animals.

Your rest

Sagittarians are energetic types who got more relaxation out of doing something than lounging around. If you ever see a Sagittarian lounging around, the chances are that their inactivity is due to being bored rigid. The ultimate Sagittarian release would be an opportunity to travel to a far-flung and unknown place with six months of freedom in which to immerse themselves in the culture; learn the language; eat, drink and laugh with the natives and trek into the foothills in search of lost temples. Such opportunities are regrettably rare, so you may have to be satisfied with pouring over maps and reading obscure travel journals that cover the same ground.

▲ Sagittarians are drawn to exotic and far-flung places. Sagittarius is, after all, the sign of the traveller.

SAGITTARIUS

132

Your health

Vigorous and athletic Sagittarians rarely suffer from illnesses for very long. Overindulgence in food or drink can be your downfall, as can accidents caused by your risk-taking.

Sickness

Your natural optimism (and fear of the negative) tends to make you underrate illnesses until they become serious. You have, however, excellent recuperative powers.

You suffer particularly from:
- Injuries resulting from sport or risky activities.
- Burns.
- Diseases associated with animals.

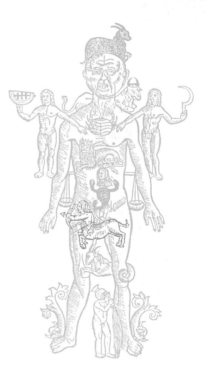

▲ A drawing from a sixteenth-century calendar shows a connection between Sagittarius and the pelvic area of the human body.

Body parts linked to Sagittarius

The parts of the body traditionally linked to the strong influence of Sagittarius are as shown on the right.

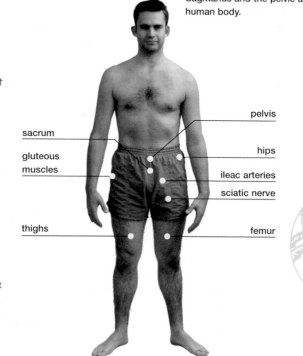

pelvis

sacrum

gluteous muscles

hips

ileac arteries

sciatic nerve

thighs

femur

▶ An individual's birth chart will show if any of these body parts have inherited a strength or vulnerability.

▶ In love

A Sagittarius in love is as obvious as a forest fire. You find it almost impossible to hide your feelings at the best of times, but when it comes to passion, your intentions shine like a beacon. The greatest danger comes from trying too hard.

Falling in love you:
- Make your intentions clear (or at least, are unable to conceal them).
- Are sincere and straightforward.
- Kick yourself every five minutes for saying something stupid.
- Feel a need to be constantly in the loved one's company.

In love you expect:
- Absolute fidelity.
- Never to have your own fidelity questioned.
- To have plenty of opportunities to laugh and have a good time.
- To retain a degree of freedom in any relationship.
- Good intellectual compatibility.

How to capture a Sagittarian's heart
- Be casual, light-hearted and, above all, witty (Sagittarians don't like heavy-handed romanticism).
- Be spontaneous, and make sure your passport is up to date.
- Don't lay down rules (Sagittarians hate to be constrained).
- Never be cruel or make jokes at the expense of others (Sagittarians are ardent humanitarians).
- Be nice to cute, furry animals.

FRIENDSHIPS AT A GLANCE

Check here for personality clashes. Friendship matches are not the same as love matches. Think about it: would you actually want to marry some of your friends?

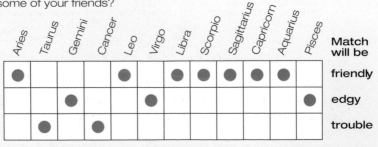

Aries	Taurus	Gemini	Cancer	Leo	Virgo	Libra	Scorpio	Sagittarius	Capricorn	Aquarius	Pisces	Match will be
●				●		●	●	●	●	●		friendly
		●			●						●	edgy
	●		●									trouble

Love matches

Aries
♈
A tremendously energetic, sexually-charged combination that will still be having a good time long after doomsday.

Taurus
♉
Sagittarius wants to see the world and collect adventures. Taurus wants to build a den and collect acorns. Difficult.

Gemini
♊
A freedom-loving couple who get on great, on the rare occasions they are in the same place at the same time.

Cancer
♋
Cancer's need to possess and cling to a lover clashes disastrously with Sagittarius's love of freedom.

Leo
♌
An enviable combination of two big hearts capable of copious love and laughter. Loyal Leos might be jealous.

Virgo
♍
An erotic timebomb waiting to happen. Outside of the bedroom though Virgo gets frustrated by the Archer's sloppy approach to life.

Libra
♎
Libra's charming magnetism is deeply attractive to Sagittarius. A very natural and easygoing pairing.

Scorpio
♏
Straightforward, good-humoured optimism meets subtlety and secretiveness. Anything could happen and probably will.

Sagittarius
♐
Two free-spirited adventurers egging each other on. Great, accept that neither of you has a clue how to be practical and it might work.

Capricorn
♑
Capricorn is touched by Sagittarius's genuine good nature, and the Archer is in awe of the Goat's maturity.

Aquarius
♒
A broad-minded, adventurous pair that will go anywhere and do anything. Your home life will be utter chaos though.

Pisces
♓
Two dreamers and idealists, but Pisces tends to be too passive and Sagittarius too blunt for sensitive fish.

SAGITTARIUS

135

▶ Sex

There is a fairly obvious reason why the symbol of Sagittarius, the archer, is half man and half beast. Couple this with the fact that Sagittarius is ruled by Jupiter, the planet of excess, and you begin to get the picture.

Your sexuality

Be extremely careful about sharing sexual fantasies with a Sagittarian lover, they have a very tenuous grasp on the distinction between fantasy and practicality and may immediately take it as an exciting suggestion rather than an intellectual excercise. The animal half of the half-man, half-beast Sagittarian libido is always switched on, but you can't ignore the human half. Sagittarians really do require as much stimulation of the mind as they do of the body for sex to be truly satisfying.

Sexual needs:

- A lover who can discuss sexual needs frankly and openly.
- Intellectual stimulation.
- A lover who can laugh in bed (especially at himself/herself).
- A lover who is graceful and gentle.
- No sexual ambiguity.

Sexual turn-ons:

- Foreigners or unusual people.
- A wide variety of energetic sexual positions.
- Sexy activities such as skinny dipping as a prelude.
- Blunt sexual talk and four-letter words.
- Orgy fantasies.

Love and sex

Sagittarians are natural spouses, though they can never quite abandon the fantasy of the one-night stand with an exotic stranger. They demand and invariably deliver fidelity, as long as they have managed to find the right partner of course. The right partner is invariably one who can treat both sex and love as a celebration.

SAGITTARIUS

136

Famous Sagittarians

22 Nov

George Eliot
Writer, 22 November 1819

George Eliot
(born 22 November 1819)

Tina Turner
Singer, 26 November 1938

26 Nov

Jimi Hendrix
(born 27 November 1942)

27 Nov

Jimi Hendrix
Musician,
27 November 1942

28 Nov

William Blake
(born 28 November 1757)

30 Nov

William Blake
Poet, artist,
28 November 1757

3 Dec

Mark Twain
Author, 30 November 1835

Mark Twain
(born 30 November 1835)

5 Dec

Sir Winston Churchill
Politician,
30 November 1874

8 Dec

Maria Callas
Opera singer,
3 December 1923

Walt Disney
(born 5 December 1901)

Walt Disney
Cartoonist,
5 December 1901

12 Dec

13 Dec

Jane Austen
(born 16 December 1775)

Sammy Davis Jr
Singer, actor,
8 December 1925

16 Dec

Frank Sinatra
Singer, 12 December 1917

Gustave Flaubert
Author, 13 December 1821

21 Dec

Jane Austen
Author, 16 December 1775

SAGITTARIUS

137

▶ Everyday life

Home is not a natural place for a Sagittarian to be. They see a home more as a convenient place to store things and sleep in between adventures.

Your home

Only those Sagittarians who have not yet figured out how to make a living while travelling the world, will be forced to find a place to call home. A Sagittarian's home, although usually charming and quirky, almost always gives the impression of being temporary. Mundane things like chairs, doors and floors are invariably blocked or buried under stacks of stuff that has been waiting to be put away for years.

Your work

A Sagittarian is the ideal person to open that new branch office in Kuala Lumpur; just don't expect them ever to come back.

Job for life?

- Research (the more obscure the subject the better).
- Anything at all to do with travel, but preferably something that involves travelling solo.
- Caring for animals (veterinary practice for example).
- Anything that is both intellectually and physically demanding.

▲ Sagittarians (22 November–21 December) are born at the traditional time of winter hunts.

Sagittarian boss

- Tends to be extremely blunt.
- Always raises a smile.
- Doesn't like dealing with the details.

Sagittarian worker

- Works fast and furiously.
- A natural morale booster.
- Has very vague career plans.
- Rarely complains.

SAGITTARIUS

Your appetites

It's a safe bet that fast food was invented by a Sagittarian. You are a sucker for all kinds of convenience foods, snacks and other unhealthy ways of stuffing your face.

It's only the amount of energy you burn up by irrepressibly dashing about that prevents you from weighing more than a house. As it is, your susceptibility to snacking probably costs you endless battles with your waistline. It isn't that you particularly enjoy low-quality foods, it's just that such foods tend to have a quality that you can't resist, namely speed. You are as impatient for the pleasures of food as you are for all other pleasures. On the positive side, this desire to eat good things 'right now' can drive you into the kitchen yourself, where you can discover your own natural talent for cooking. Your ideal meal would consist of exotic treats plucked piping hot from vendors in an oriental street market.

YOUR MONEY AND YOUR FORTUNE

You simply don't have the characteristics that are needed to get rich in business, and your capacity for spending what you don't have is breathtaking. Only Jupiter, the planet of luck, and the National Lottery can save you. To make your fortune, try these suggestions:

- Avoid get-rich-quick schemes like the plague (somebody is probably trying to rip you off).
- Open a travel agency that specializes in emu-trekking in the bush, or something equally exotic.
- Become an environmental campaigner and save the world.
- Open a restaurant that specializes in excellent food in record-breaking time.
- Find a job that requires you to travel the world sampling every type of food in existence.
- Become an entertainer and make the world a jollier place.

capricorn

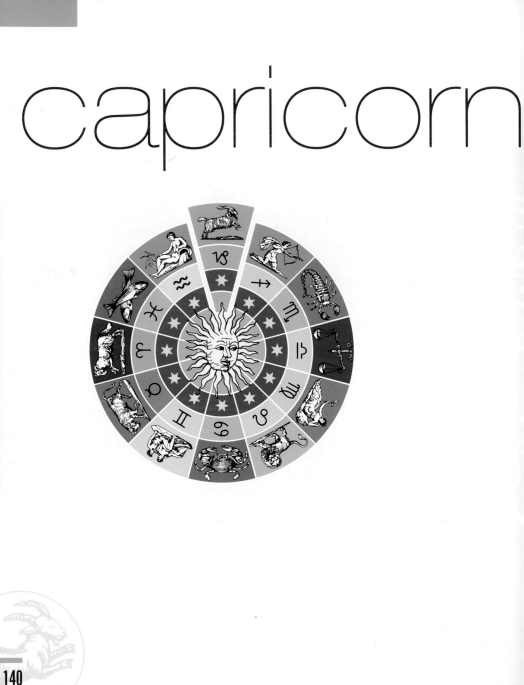

the sea-goat

22 December–19 January

Key words for Capricorn, the tenth sign of the zodiac, are:

- Realism and practicality
- Planning and persistence
- Status and quality
- Authority and discipline
- Wealth and investment
- Loyalty and wisdom
- Love and marriage

▶ Your element

Capricorn is the cardinal earth sign. Your character is unlike the other earth signs in that you are more akin to solid ground rather than any particular landscape. There is something fundamental about your character in the same way that there is something basic about a right angle; the concept is indisputable, even if you can't find any perfect examples in nature. You are a universal foundation.

▼ Saturn, ruler of structure and discipline, dominates Capricorn.

Your character

Capricorns are famous for being stable, reliable, calm and utterly dependable. You have the sure-footedness of your symbol, the sea-goat, and the tenacity to get to the top of a mountain, or the bottom of a problem, that would defeat almost anyone else. Capricorns tend to move in and make a success of things that the other, more flighty, signs have pioneered. If it weren't for Capricorns and the Capricornean spirit, nothing would ever truly be done.

Your ruling planet

Saturn, the Greek god of time, rules Capricorn. Saturn is the ruler of structure and discipline. As the most distant planet visible to the naked eye, and believed by the ancients to be the last planet, it also symbolizes limits. Saturn has a formidable reputation in astrology because it is also the planet of fear and forces confrontations with uncomfortable realities. You are likely to struggle with this (and benefit from it) all your life.

Your secrets

There is a secret and titanic struggle going on inside every Capricorn that is almost invisible from the outside. Capricorns are blessed, and cursed, with a tremendous clear perception of the real world. The reason Capricorns call a spade a spade, is because they can clearly see that is exactly what it is. It can be painful to have to face reality in such an unfiltered way, and this is a pain that Capricorns feel for much of their lives. Only age and experience can help them come to terms with it.

CAPRICORN

142

CHARACTERISTICS
POSITIVE

- Totally realistic
- Give excellent advice
- Highly responsible
- Immensely productive
- Relentless
- Strategically brilliant
- Self-disciplined
- Natural leader
- Dignified

NEGATIVE

- Extremely conservative
- Workaholic
- Fearful and repressed
- Pessimistic
- Easily discouraged
- Inhibited
- Sarcastic

LUCKY CONNECTIONS

Colours	Green, black, grey, indigo, violet
Plants	Yew, ash, hemp, weeping willow
Perfume	Musk
Gemstones	Jet, black diamond, onyx, ruby
Metal	Lead
Tarot card	The devil
Animals	Goat, ass

LIFE

New GIs in Vietnam: commanding them in the old way is out

Look out – he's back

A different Muhammad Ali returns to the ring

3/-

SPARTAK

NOVEMBER 9 · 1970

◄ Muhammad Ali (born 17 January 1942) displayed the typical Capricornean qualities of self-discipline and strategic thinking in the ring, and Capricorn's natural dignity and leadership qualities outside of it.

The man

These are typical characteristics of the Capricorn male, but they are by no means universal. Strong influences in an individual's birth chart, such as the positions of the planets, can distort or skew these characteristics, but they are rarely altogether absent.

Typical appearance
- Stocky build.
- Shorter than average.
- Penetrating eyes.
- Very strong teeth.
- Looks older than his years.
- Swift and purposeful movements.

Personality
- Dignified manner.
- Strong opinions.
- Very polite.
- Direct and never condescending.
- Avoids the limelight.
- Uncomfortable talking about feelings.
- A little repressed and prudish.
- Difficult to approach.
- Rarely smiles.

▲ The planet Saturn rules in both Capricorn and Aquarius.

YOUNG CAPRICORN

The child
The typical Capricorn child:
- Looks very mature.
- Has great respect for authority.
- Likes the company of adults.
- Is self-contained and strong-willed.
- Always gets what he/she wants.
- Has only one or two close friends.
- Likes doing practical things.
- Is fascinated by clocks.
- Is even-tempered.
- Has an infallible memory.

The woman

These are typical characteristics of the Capricorn female, but they are by no means universal. Strong influences in an individual's birth chart, such as the positions of the planets, can distort or skew these characteristics, but they are rarely altogether absent.

Typical appearance

- Small and trim figure.
- Inclined to frown.
- Looks older when young, and younger when old.
- Slender neck.
- Full mouth and very white teeth.
- Shapely legs and small feet.

Personality

- Very self-conscious.
- Appears stable, but can be moody.
- Finds domesticity boring.
- Hates to be made fun of.
- Rarely smiles.
- Excellent dress sense.
- Very loyal to friends and family.
- Difficult to approach.

Parenting a young Capricorn

Young Capricorns can sometimes seem like the proverbial old soul in a young body. Nothing pleases them more than appearing to be grown up and responsible. In extreme cases, young Capricorns have been known to wear ties and to eschew hide-and-seek in the garden in favour of joining the adults for a chat over coffee. Parents of a Capricorn must remember that this is only an act. A child is still a child, no matter how grown-up he/she likes to appear. They are still prey to the same irrational fears and need the same unconditional love that all children need.

At school, young Capricorn tends to excel at gaining titles, prizes and certificates, even in subjects that they have no special talent for. Parents shouldn't worry if their young Sea-Goat seems to have only one or two friends, Capricorns are just built that way.

▶ Your leisure

LOVES AND HATES

You love

- Reliability and professionalism.
- Finishing what you start.
- Putting things on the firmest possible foundations.
- Having a clear purpose.
- Privacy.

You hate

- Hare-brained schemes.
- People who don't finish what they start.
- Rudeness and crudity.
- Being made to look a fool.

Strategy and tactics are the only elements of sport that hold any real attraction for you. You tend to be disciplined about taking exercise, but really prefer intellectual pursuits.

Hobbies and pastimes

Looking for a hobby? Try one of these:

- Tactical games (chess is an obvious example).
- Playing or listening to music.
- Museums and galaries (you have a rare affinity with the past).
- Archaeology.
- Hiking and rambling (you like having time to think in an unhurried environment).
- Collecting or repairing clocks and watches.

Your rest

You find social occasions something of a strain, unless you know the people present very well. Parties are not really your scene because you don't like the false facades that people put on. Mental stimulation is much more your style when it comes to leisure.

Many Capricorns have immensely ambitious hobby projects that they spend years perfecting. These are often kept private, and may seem like obsessions to other, less tenacious, individuals. You have a fascination with history and the passing of time so archaeological ruins and museums of antiquities are often favourite haunts. Capricorns tend to become much more relaxed and easy-going once they get beyond the age of forty.

▲ Capricorns enjoy unhurried rambles, preferably with a bit of historical interest, and definitely with a very close friend.

Your health

Capricorns have a reputation for living to a ripe old age. This is down to their conservative, stable approach to life and their connection with Saturn, the ancient god of time.

Sickness

Worry, pessimism and overwork tend to be Capricorn's downfall. Curiously, you seem to become more and more resistant to illness the older you get. You suffer particularly from:

● Rheumatism and bone disease.
● Skin problems.
● Problems with legs and knees.

▲ A sixteenth-century calendar shows a connection between Capricorn and the knees.

Body parts linked to Capricorn

The parts of the body traditionally linked to the strong influence of Capricorn are as shown on the right.

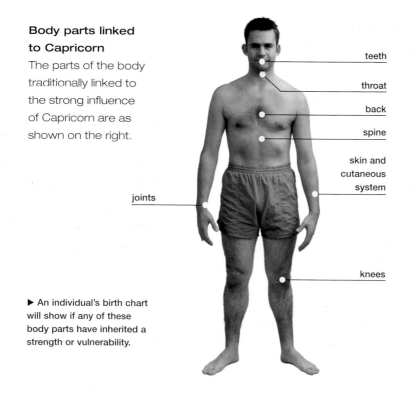

teeth

throat

back

spine

skin and cutaneous system

joints

knees

▶ An individual's birth chart will show if any of these body parts have inherited a strength or vulnerability.

▶ In love

Capricorn's natural caution reaches absurd levels when it comes to love. Capricorns are very wary of opening themselves up at the best of times, and when it comes to something as intimate as love they are more carefully guarded than George Bush in a war zone.

Falling in love you:
- Think very long and very hard before committing yourself.
- Use charm to hide your discomfort.
- Are very easily put off by teasing (even if done jokingly).
- Find it very difficult to open yourself up.

In love you expect:
- Long-term commitment.
- Your lover to know that you love them without having to repeat it every five minutes.
- Your private life to be kept strictly private.
- To work hard for emotional and financial security.

How to capture a Capricorn's heart
- Be classy and have impeccable manners.
- Don't expect blatant flirtation to get you anywhere.
- Be extremely patient (Capricorns never do anything without thinking about it long and hard first, or if they do they regret it).
- Avoid sloppy romanticism.
- Be prepared for a surprise when you finally get him/her into the bedroom.

FRIENDSHIPS AT A GLANCE

Check here for personality clashes. Friendship matches are not the same as love matches. Think about it: would you actually want to marry some of your friends?

Aries	Taurus	Gemini	Cancer	Leo	Virgo	Libra	Scorpio	Sagittarius	Capricorn	Aquarius	Pisces	Match will be
	●				●		●	●	●	●	●	friendly
●			●			●						edgy
		●		●								trouble

Love matches

Extreme cases

Aries ♈ Capricorn may initially be excited by Aries' wildness, but will soon tire of their hare-brained schemes. ✗

Taurus ♉ Two characters with strong and complementary views on the value of security, wealth and sex. ✓

Gemini ♊ Gemini's quick, sometimes cruel, laughter will tend to wound sensitive Capricorn deeply. ✗

Cancer ♋ You share an appreciation of family and tradition and Cancer can give the unconditional love that Capricorn needs.

Leo ♌ Both adore luxury and the good things in life, but Capricorn finds Leo's grandiose gestures a little tiresome.

Virgo ♍ An endlessly congenial and supportive coupling that works hard and has natural rapport. ✓

Libra ♎ Manners, good taste and refined romance appeal to both, but neither are much good at identifying emotional strains.

Scorpio ♏ A lusty and powerful combination. This is a pair that could conquer the world as long as they stick together. ✓

Sagittarius ♐ Irrepressible optimism meets realistic pessimism. Perhaps there is a chance of balance for both.

Capricorn ♑ Shared ambitions and tastes are in your favour, but there is little time for fun and possible depression looms large.

Aquarius ♒ Cosmic opposites and natural enemies. Capricorn is the rule-maker, Aquarius is the rule-breaker. Little chance of success. ✗

Pisces ♓ Piscean escapism is one of the few forces in the universe that can beguile and soothe Capricorn. ✓

▶ Sex

Capricornean lustiness is one of the world's best-kept secrets. This is partly down to Capricorn's cool and collected exterior, but mostly due to the extreme care with which Capricorns conceal their inner natures.

Your sexuality

People often forget you are an earth sign, and that means you have an intuitive grasp of the pleasures of the body. What really makes you a spectacular, if hard to get, lover though is your dislike of leaving things half done. Quickie sex is foreign to your nature. Your view is 'if you are going to do it, do it right.' Total satisfaction, for you and your partner, is your goal. You like order and a no-nonsense approach to your sex life and you have enviable stamina once aroused.

Sexual needs:
- A strong and direct approach.
- A lover who is comfortable with your power.
- A lover who knows how to be powerful.
- Excellent manners and considerate lovemaking.
- Mental stimulation.

Sexual turn-ons:
- Having power.
- Submitting to power.
- The idea of love.
- Being nurtured.
- A lover who knows what you want without discussion.
- Realistic eroticism.
- Being allowed to let go.

Love and sex

Capricorns are the only people in the world who really truly believe that love and sex are inseparable. The extreme care with which they tend to select sexual partners reflects this fact. As in other areas of their lives, Capricorns become more and more comfortable with sex, and with love, as they grow older.

Famous Capricorns

22 Dec

24 Dec

Ava Gardner
Actress, 24 December 1922

25 Dec

Annie Lennox
Singer, 25 December 1954

26 Dec

27 Dec

Mao Tse-Tung
Chinese politician,
26 December 1893

Marlene Dietrich
Actress, 27 December 1901

Isaac Newton
Scientist, 4 January 1643

4 Jan

Saint Joan of Arc
French heroine,
6 January 1412

6 Jan

Elvis Presley
Singer, 8 January 1935

8 Jan

9 Jan

David Bowie
Singer, 8 January 1947

Simone de Beauvoir
Author, 9 January 1908

14 Jan

Dr Albert Schweitzer
Missionary and author,
14 January 1875

15 Jan

17 Jan

Martin Luther King
Civil rights leader,
15 January 1929

20 Jan

**Muhammad Ali
(Cassius Clay)**
Boxer, 17 January 1942

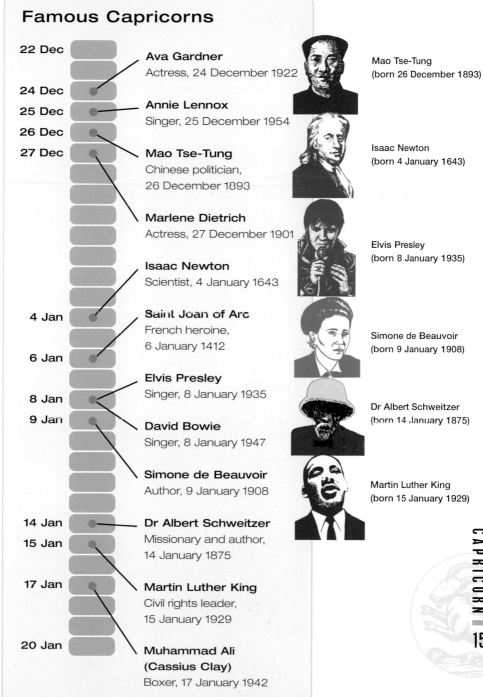

Mao Tse-Tung
(born 26 December 1893)

Isaac Newton
(born 4 January 1643)

Elvis Presley
(born 8 January 1935)

Simone de Beauvoir
(born 9 January 1908)

Dr Albert Schweitzer
(born 14 January 1875)

Martin Luther King
(born 15 January 1929)

CAPRICORN

151

▶ Everyday life

Capricorn has a deeply conservative nature, and it tends to show in their homes. The decor tends to be seriously out of date and the furniture and fittings are far from cutting edge. Capricorns always have a favourite chair.

Your home

There is a conflict between your love of luxury and the less than glamorous appearance of your home. This is because, for you, luxury has little to do with how much something costs and a lot to do with how well it does its job. You would rather have a battered old clock that keeps perfect time than a rare and expensive antique that regularly goes haywire.

Your work

Capricorns probably form the backbone of every major industry in the world. They are also natural and competent leaders.

Job for life?

- Politics.
- Banking.
- Any job that requires good organizational skills and takes place behind the scenes.
- Antique restorer.
- Historian or archaeologist.
- Property developer.
- Architect or builder.

▲ Capricorneans (22 December–19 January) are born as the winter turns, traditionally a time of rejoicing and feasts.

CAPRICORN

152

Capricornean boss
- Always sees things through to the end.
- Inspires loyalty, but rarely friendship.

Capricornean worker
- Can be domineering.
- Is extremely dependable.
- Always seeks to become more powerful.

Your appetites

Capricorns have a penchant for home-cooked food. Not only does it tend to be simple and honest fare, it also allows them to spend time with their families, where they love to be.

You cannot abide the notion of paying extravagant sums of money for tiny portions of fashionable cuisine. A plateful of meat and two veg without pretentiousness is the ideal dish to set before a Capricorn. Those Capricorns whose tastes are a little more adventurous tend to be fascinated by historical recipes. Traditional Victorian Christmas puddings, cooked with strictly nineteenth-century ingredients, might appeal to you. When it comes to drink you are strictly Old World in your wine tastes, and you believe there is probably nothing in the world that is better for you than a traditional pint of beer.

YOUR MONEY AND YOUR FORTUNE

Money interests you less than power, which you pursue ruthlessly. Fortunately, one tends to bring the other, so you are on to a winner. Many captains of industry are Capricorns. Your dedication and unflinching realism tend to carry you naturally to the top. To make your fortune try these suggestions:

- Stop worrying, it will probably never happen.
- Write a best-selling sex manual (under a pseudonym).
- Record everything anybody says to you so you can back up your infallible memory with proof.
- Become a feared arts critic.
- Come up with a way of achieving peace in the Middle East (an organizational challenge worthy of your talents).
- Start charging for financial advice.

aquarius

the water-carrier

20 January–18 February

Key words for Aquarius, the eleventh sign of the zodiac, are:

- Imagination and inventiveness
- Kindness and humanitarianism
- Independence and detachment
- Warmth and friendship
- Quirkiness and rebellion
- Analysis and experimentation
- Mystery and originality

▶ Your element

Aquarius is the fixed air sign. Air represents pure thought and the mind, so Aquarians excel at original thinking and positively bulge with unusual ideas. Unfortunately they tend to produce as many utterly impractical concepts as they do useful innovations. Aquarians are the rebels of the zodiac and they love to burst boundaries. They therefore tend to be extremely sceptical about astrology.

▼ Uranus, master of the unexpected, and Saturn, ruler of time and wisdom, both rule Aquarius.

Your character

You will usually be sympathetic to others but, though kind and friendly, you can frequently be unpredictable and sometimes a little distant. Independence is important to you, even at the cost of personal relationships. This may make it difficult for people to feel really close to you. They may find you contrary and eccentric. You can be a keen campaigner for causes you support and will not worry if more conventional people disagree with you. Race, class and age create no barriers for you. You tend to be high-principled and egalitarian and may have a bent towards science and technology. Although more comfortable with ideas than emotions you are congenial in company.

Your ruling planet

Both Uranus and Saturn rule Aquarius. Uranus is primarily the planet of the unexpected and the unusual, and Saturn the planet linked to the ability to apply wisdom and to plan ahead. Aquarians tend to be original thinkers and to be highly analytical, giving them a combination of imagination and clear-headedness.

Your secrets

However clever or artistically talented you are, and despite the appearance you present to the world, you may lack self-confidence. Aquarians are often very uncertain of their true identity: you may find your ego very precarious, perhaps because of your nonconforming nature. Make practical use of your ability to attract friends, and of your intellectual abilities to build up an identifiable ego. Avoid pointless rebellion and don't rely on an eccentric hairstyle to distinguish yourself.

AQUARIUS

156

CHARACTERISTICS
POSITIVE

- Thoughtful and caring
- Good communicator
- Loyal and dependable
- Inventive
- Altruistic

- Humanitarian idealist
- Think independently
- Interested in people
- Scientific mind

NEGATIVE

- Perverse and eccentric
- Lacking in confidence
- Nosily curious
- Rude and tactless
- Wilfully contrary

- Casually thoughtless
- Self-centred
- Secretive, especially with your ideas

LUCKY CONNECTIONS

Colours	Electric blue and light yellow
Plants	Orchids, olive and aspen
Perfume	Galbanum
Gemstone	Amethyst
Metal	Lead
Tarot card	The star
Animals	Eagle and peacock

◀ James Dean, (born 8 February 1931) has come to represent the epitome of the nonchalant youthful rebel. Rebelliousness and free-thinking are both typical Aquarian traits.

JAMES DEAN

A Biography
By
WILLIAM BAST

The brilliant young actor's art and life—told by the man who knew him best.

AQUARIUS

The man

These are typical characteristics of the Aquarius male, but they are by no means universal. Strong influences in an individual's birth chart, such as the positions of the planets, can distort or skew these characteristics, but they are rarely altogether absent.

Typical appearance
- Taller than average height.
- Long boned, often with broad hips.
- Regular features with a broad forehead.
- Handsome rather than distinctive.
- A fleshy and softened jawline.
- In thought head drops forward or sideways.
- Eyes often look distant and dreamy.
- Movement purposeful rather than graceful.

Personality
- Friendly and gregarious, but can be stubborn.
- Fair-minded with a strong personal moral code.
- Drawn to the arcane and secret.
- Thinks intuitively but with a streak of practicality.
- Keeps his own feelings to himself.
- Interested in developing his ideas more than making a profit from them.

▲ The planet Saturn rules in both Aquarius and Capricorn.

YOUNG AQUARIUS

The child
The typical Aquarius child:
- Is quick-thinking, sensitive and intuitive.
- Seems confident, relaxed and charming.
- Is full of ideas, sometimes zany ones.
- Wants to analyse everything.
- Is generous to his/her many friends.
- Feels pressured by emotional demands.
- May rebel against rules and discipline, but is sensible when allowed to work things out rationally.

AQUARIUS

158

The woman

These are typical characteristics of the Aquarius female, but they are by no means universal. Strong influences in an individual's birth chart, such as the positions of the planets, can distort or skew these characteristics, but they are rarely altogether absent.

Typical appearance

- May have broad shoulders.
- Bone structure tends to be large.
- Long and graceful neck.
- Lively eyes.
- Wide and expressive mouth.
- Dresses unconventionally.

Personality

- Can be very unpredictable.
- Lacks self-confidence.
- Tolerant and accepting of others.
- Good at settling other people's arguments.
- Wide interests.
- Sure of her own mind.
- Active and concerned in community affairs.
- Has many and varied friends.

Parenting a young Aquarian

Their enquiring and analytical minds keep young Aquarians always on the go. They need to be given plenty of opportunity to make discoveries, experiment with inventions and present their burgeoning ideas, but remember that they may find close relationships difficult and seem detached. They are very sensitive to domestic tension and disruption and need a peaceful and harmonious environment. To build the young water-carrier's confidence he or she needs plenty of encouragement.

Perhaps because their minds work so quickly, young Aquarians sometimes get themselves into a muddle. Help them to develop logical thinking and ways of training their memory. Teach them how to find their way back to you if they should ever get lost.

▶ Your leisure

LOVES AND HATES

- Fame and recognition.
- Change, surprises and the unusual or odd.
- Eccentric friends.
- Privacy.
- Giving orders.

You hate

- Violence of all kinds.
- Show-offs.
- People taking you for granted.
- Borrowing or lending.
- People trying to pin you down to a decision.

Adventurous, and unusual, airborne activities such as flying, gliding and parachuting are perhaps more to your taste than conventional sports. Local politics and social and third world charities may be things to which you give your spare time.

Hobbies and pastimes

If you are looking for a hobby then why not try

- Theatre and creative arts.
- Playing an instrument.
- Dance or aerobics.
- Clowning, juggling, stand-up comedy.
- Magic and tricks.
- Personal writing: a journal or autobiography.
- Weight training or other controlled exercise.

Your rest

Aquarians really know how to take it easy and you will enjoy taking time out and doing nothing. You are never happier than when relaxing in a hammock in the garden, reading by the swimming pool, cosy at home listening to music or just dreaming the day away. On holiday, however, you may also like to exercise your mind and satisfy your inquisitive nature, exploring new places, looking at architecture and visiting galleries, where you are likely to prefer more modern art, or perhaps working on an archaeological dig.

▲ Aquarians relish the sense of freedom that an unusual and individual sport such as parachuting can provide.

Your health

You need plenty of fresh air, sleep and regular exercise but many Aquarians fail to ensure they have enough of these. You have little resistance to excessive heat, cold or humidity.

Sickness

Most young Aquarians are very healthy, having only the occasional complaint that goes away without doing anything in particular about it. Hyperactive mental work may lead to nervous complaints or phobias.

You may particularly suffer from:

● Circulatory problems.
● Varicose veins.
● Diseases of the blood and nervous system.
● Accidents to the calves and ankles.

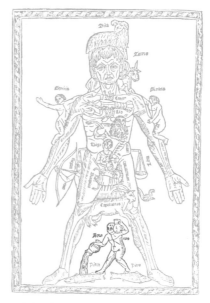

▲ A drawing from a sixteenth-century calendar shows a connection between Aquarius and the lower legs.

Body parts linked to Aquarius

The parts of the body traditionally linked to the strong influence of Aquarius are as shown on the right.

▶ An individual's birth chart will show if any of these body parts have inherited a strength or vulnerability.

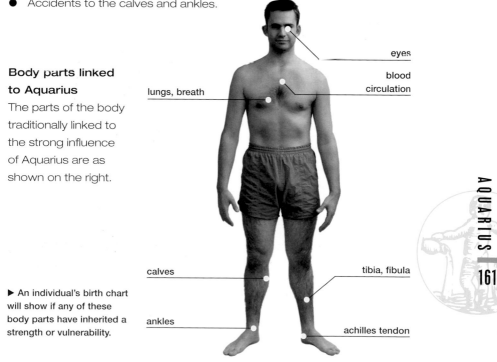

eyes

blood circulation

lungs, breath

calves

tibia, fibula

ankles

achilles tendon

▶ In love

Aquarians are keener on the idea of love than the reality. They easily feel trapped and may be more comfortable living alone. In the right relationship, Aquarians are very stable but their dispassionate natures can cause conflict.

Falling in love you:
- Are likely to attract by your friendly manner.
- Are afraid of deep attachments.
- Develop a relationship slowly.
- Need space to assert your independence.
- May find a live-apart arrangement preferable to cohabiting.

In love you expect:
- Tolerance and understanding, especially of personal eccentricities.
- Monogamy and loyalty.
- To continue to see a wide circle of friends, men and women.
- No constraints on your personal freedom.
- No displays of jealousy.

How to capture an Aquarian's heart
- Take things very slowly at first.
- Show you can be a good friend before trying to become a lover.
- Do not make emotional demands but respond gently to theirs.
- Let them dominate the partnership.
- Show how tolerant you are.

FRIENDSHIPS AT A GLANCE

Check here for personality clashes. Friendship matches are not the same as love matches. Think about it: would you actually want to marry some of your friends?

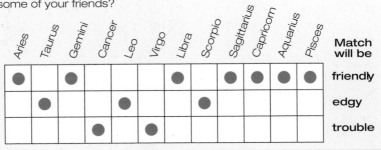

Aries	Taurus	Gemini	Cancer	Leo	Virgo	Libra	Scorpio	Sagittarius	Capricorn	Aquarius	Pisces	Match will be
●		●				●		●	●	●	●	friendly
	●		●				●					edgy
				●	●							trouble

Love matches

Extreme cases

Aries ♈ Brash bold Aries is too here-and-now for the forward-looking, thoughtful Aquarian.

Taurus ♉ Down-to-earth and sensual Taureans are not a good match for cool, stargazing Aquarians.

Gemini ♊ An ideal match but neither of you are emotional beings so it won't be passion that keeps you together. ♥

Cancer ♋ Warm nurturing Cancer might be too smothering for the Water-Carrier's cool temperament.

Leo ♌ Fixed fire and fixed air are surprisingly compatible as long as Leo gets enough attention.

Virgo ♍ Plenty to talk about but very different emotionally. More suited to a business than romantic relationship. ✗

Libra ♎ Both very private, fond of magic and secret things, they have plenty to share and connect well mentally.

Scorpio ♏ Fundamental opposites, and stubborn ones at that. Scorpio needs emotional nurturing and attachment. ✗

Sagittarius ♐ Be prepared to live on take-aways and pizzas and hire a cleaner. A brilliant but chaotic pair.

Capricorn ♑ The traditional authoritarian meets the archetypal rebel. Almost certainly a recipe for disaster. ✗

Aquarius ♒ Unorthodoxy rules this match, but emotional problems might leave you stranded on opposite shores.

Pisces ♓ Pisces and Aquarius share altruism but Pisceans are too sensitive for cool, detached Aquarius.

▶ Sex

Aquarians are curious about everything and hate the concept of taboos. Consequently they tend to be extremely inventive and rather kinky lovers.

Your sexuality

You tend to be very faithful yourself but you are not possessive and unlikely to be very jealous. Your partner may worry that you are seeing other people but the chances are that you will just be talking, rather than being physically unfaithful. However, you are not very good at listening to your partner's emotional problems, and verbal quarrels may take the place of physical contact. You love to explore boundaries, so you need a lover with nerves of steel and a complete lack of physical hang-ups.

Sexual needs:
- No heavy emotional demands.
- Not to feel pressured.
- A lover who will still make you feel in control.
- To work up to things slowly.
- Lots of physical stimulation.
- Imaginative lovemaking.
- Untrammelled abandonment when ready for it.

Sexual turn-ons:
- Erotic conversation, but be wary that the talk doesn't become more important than the lovemaking.
- Openly offered stimulation without sentimentality.
- Exploring different erotic zones.
- Role-playing, provided you can call the shots if you want to.

Love and sex

Aquarians' strong independent streak and avoidance of heavy emotional scenes often means that you have many brief affairs before eventually finding a partner. Holiday flings and weekends on the beach may play a big part in your love life. You are more likely to permit yourself a sexual response with the person who offers an imaginative date or an unusual location.

In memory dear, My Valentine.

AQUARIUS

164

Famous Aquarians

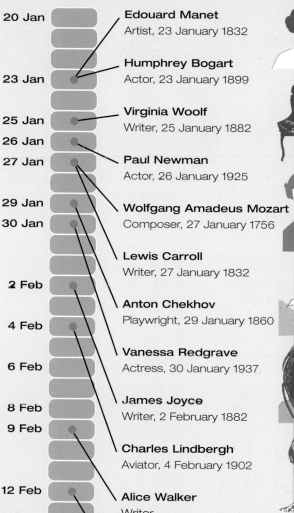

20 Jan	**Edouard Manet** Artist, 23 January 1832
23 Jan	**Humphrey Bogart** Actor, 23 January 1899
25 Jan	**Virginia Woolf** Writer, 25 January 1882
26 Jan	**Paul Newman** Actor, 26 January 1925
27 Jan	**Wolfgang Amadeus Mozart** Composer, 27 January 1756
29 Jan	**Lewis Carroll** Writer, 27 January 1832
30 Jan	**Anton Chekhov** Playwright, 29 January 1860
	Vanessa Redgrave Actress, 30 January 1937
2 Feb	**James Joyce** Writer, 2 February 1882
4 Feb	**Charles Lindbergh** Aviator, 4 February 1902
6 Feb	**Alice Walker** Writer, 9 February 1944
8 Feb	**Charles Darwin** Naturalist, 12 February 1809
9 Feb	**Yoko Ono** Pop artist, 18 February 1933
12 Feb	
18 Feb	

Virginia Woolf
(born 25 January 1882)

Wolfgang Amadeus
Mozart
(born 27 January 1756)

Lewis Carroll
(born 27 January 1832)

Charles Lindbergh
(born 4 February 1902)

Alice Walker
(born 9 February 1944)

Charles Darwin
(born 12 February 1809)

▶ Everyday life

You are almost certainly not domestic by nature and you are unlikely to be a cosy home-maker, but home is nevertheless a place where you can express your unconventionality. Aquarians tend to be either sophisticated or rather messy.

Your home

On the one hand you may have an elegant, spacious home with a well-displayed collection of interesting and unusual objects and artworks you have collected, where you enjoy having house-guests and giving parties. If you are the other kind of Aquarian, you probably live in a tiny, untidy apartment which is crammed with oddities.

Your work

You like investigative, analytical work with plenty of variety and enjoy working as part of a group.

Job for life?

- TV or radio presenter.
- Work with international aid organizations and charities.
- Archaeology or forensics.
- You may change jobs quite frequently at first and even make a complete career change in later life.

▲ Aquarians (20 January–18 February) are born during scarcity, when animals must be fed on the previous year's harvest.

Aquarian boss

- A fair employer.
- Rewards extra effort and input.
- Does not tolerate dishonesty.
- Quick-thinking and analytical.

Aquarian worker

- Is conscientious and reliable.
- Does not like decision making.
- Better at creative work than a routine job.

Your appetites

It is unlikely that the average Aquarian will be particularly interested in cooking; they prefer to eat out whenever they get the chance. As with their home environment, the water-carriers divide into two quite different types:

On the one hand you may be keen on exotic and unusual foods, even going so far as to seek out new gourmet recipes, especially if you can get someone else to cook them. On the other you may be a stickler for plain cooking; meat and two veg, or pie and mash, but often with unusual accompaniments. Whichever you are, your analytic nature may make you very aware of maintaining a healthy balanced diet, and making sure you get all the right minerals and vitamins.

YOUR MONEY AND YOUR FORTUNE

Ideas and inventiveness are a great asset to a business but you must investigate the way a business operates and gives as much effort to running it if you are to make it successful. Aquarians do not make the most reliable breadwinners; rather than stick to a boring routine, they always want to try something new. Follow these suggestions to make your fortune:

- Make your mark in computer graphics or run a website.
- Exploit your geniality and calm demeanour as a talk-show host.
- Join one of the world's environmental organizations and save the planet.
- Try social work but avoid counselling: you are not the best of listeners.
- Don't just have ideas, think about how you can exploit them.
- Remember: fame doesn't pay the bills, you have to put it to use.

pisces

the fishes

19 Febuary–20 March

Key words for Pisces, the twelfth sign of the zodiac, are:

- Compassion and altruism
- Wisdom and memory
- Art and performance
- Sensitivity and psychic powers
- Fantasy and emotion
- Intuition and humour
- Hidden depths and sudden storms

▶ Your element

Pisces is the mutable water sign of the zodiac. Pisceans are as changeable as water, which can become in turn clouds, rain, hail and snow. It is an element of sudden storms, shifting currents and great calms. With this changeability however can also come confusion and indecision. You are very sensitive and adaptable but can sometimes be a little too unworldly and impractical for the modern world. Over the centuries, many of the world's great artists and performers have been Pisceans.

▼ Jupiter and Neptune, the rulers of expansion and dreams respectively, rule Pisces.

Your character

Pisces can veer between extremes; it is not by chance their sign is two fishes. You can rise to the challenges of life and reach the heights, or take the easy solution to life's problems by doing nothing and sinking into oblivion. You are likely to have great compassion for others, sometimes shown in practical ways such as nursing but also in more spiritual ways through prayer and meditation. If you are going to swim to the top you need to find peace in yourself and will gain this through music, beauty and spiritual harmony.

Your ruling planet

Two planets rule Pisces: Jupiter and Neptune. Jupiter is the planet of expansion. It is linked with the hierarchies of the Church and Law and (especially conjoined with Neptune) philanthropic institutions. Neptune reigns over dreams and fantasies, of glamour and illusion. It also rules the unconscious. If you can stop dreaming and bring yourself into the real world, the influence of these planets on Pisces will help you to bring benefit to others through your sensitivity.

Your secrets

Your greatest problem is that life offers you choice and with your changeability comes indecision. Make the right choices and you will go far. If you are going to turn your private dreams and aspirations into reality you will have to emerge from fantasy land and live in the practical everyday world of work. Luckily, your sign brings many talents to help you succeed in the caring professions or in arts and entertainment. But you must face up to things and not rely on winning big in Vegas.

CHARACTERISTICS

POSITIVE

- Sensitive and sympathetic
- Imaginative
- Creative
- Generous and hospitable
- Loving and caring
- Romantic
- Artistic
- Painfully shy
- Inherently mystical

NEGATIVE

- Weak and indecisive
- Temperamental and sensationalist
- Lethargic and depressive
- Over-dependent and emotionally vulnerable
- Self-pitying
- Vague and careless

LUCKY CONNECTIONS

Colours	Lavender, sea-green, blue
Plants	Lotus and other waterplants, opium poppy
Perfume	Ambergris
Gemstones	Pearl, aquamarine, amethyst
Metal	Tin
Tarot card	The Moon
Animals	Dolphin, fishes

February 23, 1992

NEWS OF THE WORLD MAGAZINE

Sunday

The world's most beautiful woman Liz Taylor turns 60

LEAP YEAR SPECIAL
Girls make him an offer he can't refuse

AMAZING OFFER
A free gold bracelet for you

◄ Elizabeth Taylor, (born 27 February 1932) once dubbed 'the world's most beautiful woman' and famed for her potrayal of the mysteriously alluring Queen Cleopatra, is a Piscean.

The man

These are typical characteristics of the Pisces male, but they are by no means universal. Strong influences in an individual's birth chart, such as the positions of the planets, can distort or skew these characteristics, but they are rarely altogether absent.

Typical appearance

- Usually quite short and thickset.
- Can be tall, though not imposing.
- Often broad-shouldered.
- Overall may appear rather clumsy.
- Oddly shaped head with large jowls.
- Sleepy-looking eyes and large eyebrows.
- Limbs generally short.
- Movement purposeful rather than graceful.

Personality

- Emotionally involved in whatever he does.
- Lacking in prejudice.
- Rarely jealous but easily hurt.
- Romantic and a dreamer.
- Needs few material possessions.
- Unambitious, though making good use of lucky opportunities.
- Unconcerned by status of others or for himself.

▲ The planet Jupiter rules in both Pisces and Sagittarius.

YOUNG PISCES

The child

The typical Pisces child:

- Has a happy disposition: temper tantrums are very rare.
- Is imaginative and sometimes seems to be living in a secret world.
- Believes in fairies and Santa Claus.
- Dislikes strict discipline.
- Likes being with adults rather than with other children.
- Needs lots of stable emotional connections.

The woman

These are typical characteristics of the Pisces female, but they are by no means universal. Strong influences in an individual's birth chart, such as the positions of the planets, can distort or skew these characteristics, but they are rarely altogether absent.

Typical appearance

- Usually slim.
- Oval face with full cheeks.
- An ethereal look with an air of mystery.
- Small nose and pointed chin.
- Large round eyes with arched eyebrows.
- Generous and sensual mouth with a charming smile.

Personality

- Warm and sympathetic.
- Devoted to others.
- Wants to belong, to a group or to a partner.
- Vague and dreamy manner.
- May appear helpless but subtlety gets things organized.
- Hides her vulnerability with sophistication.

Parenting a young Piscean

Piscean children become very attached to people rather than toys or places so take care they do not become too clingy. Encourage their self-confidence. They are passive and do not push themselves forward. Do not force them into leaderships roles, especially at school; they will not be happy as class monitor or captain of the football team. With their imagination and creativity they can dream up wonderful games but will be happy for other children to take the lead. They may need guidance to separate their fantasies from reality and help in learning to cope with bullying to which their pacific nature may make them vulnerable. Help them to become more practical or they may grow up very untidy and always late for things. Be careful not to spoil them. They take in facts and ideas quickly and are often good at foreign languages.

▶ Your leisure

LOVES AND HATES

You love
- Artistic pursuits.
- Candlelight and romantic places.
- Films, theatre and magicians.
- Poetry and fantasy fiction.
- Sailing into the sunset.

You hate
- Violence of all kinds.
- Ugly places and objects.
- Noise and overcrowding.
- Authoritarianism.
- Starched clothing.

Leisure is a time for Pisces to escape from practicalities to a world where you can live your dreams, if not always in practice then through books, films and plays as well as your imagination.

Hobbies and pastimes
Looking for a hobby? Try one of these:
- Dance classes.
- Painting and print-making.
- Poetry and creative writing.
- Figure skating.
- Water-skiing and gentler watersports.
- Motor racing.
- Sky-diving or hand gliding.

Your rest
With your fertile imagination you can turn a walk in a snowstorm into an expedition to the North Pole so it is no surprise that you can be perfectly happy curled up with a book in front of a log fire, relaxing in the countryside and just letting your mind wander, or listening to music with a glass of wine.

With your romantic mind and all the information that you squirrel away you'll feel just as refreshed by exploring an old castle and bringing it to life, or experiencing the tranquillity of a temple or sacred site.

Perfect for some Pisceans is gliding, moving gently on the air currents, looking down on houses, ships, rivers, beaches and rolling landscape from a peaceful separate world.

▲ Pisceans are fascinated by spirituality and religion. They love exploring temples and shrines.

PISCES
174

Your health

It doesn't take much to make a Piscean depressed so you may be at risk from this but if you are loved and happy you usually have no major health problems.

Sickness

Depression or the Piscean attraction to fantasy can sometimes lead to problems with alcohol or substance abuse, especially at times of emotional insecurity.

You may particularly suffer from:

- Stress-related conditions.
- Nervous disorders.
- Bunions, corns, chilblains.
- Alcoholism.

▲ A sixteenth-century calendar shows a connection between Pisces and the feet.

Body parts linked to Pisces

The parts of the body traditionally linked to the strong influence of Pisces are as shown on the right.

▶ An individual's birth chart will show if any of these body parts have inherited a strength or vulnerability.

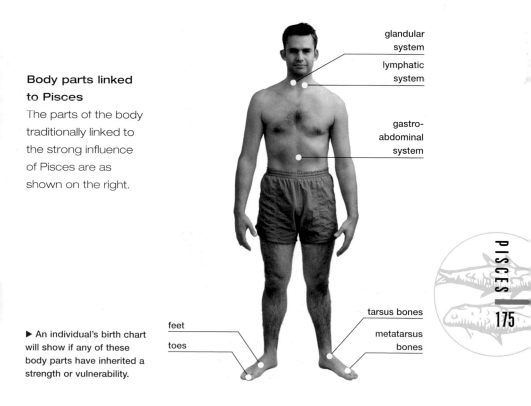

glandular system

lymphatic system

gastro-abdominal system

tarsus bones

metatarsus bones

feet

toes

▶ In love

You are a sentimental romantic dreaming of that stranger you are going to meet and spend the rest of your life with by the side of a blue lagoon. Be careful you don't project the fantasy onto an entirely unsuitable canvas.

Falling in love you:
- Can easily be swept off your feet.
- Are easily emotionally involved and easily deceived.
- Feel that together you can stand all life can throw at you.
- Adapt to what the relationship demands.
- Need constant reassurance.
- Are easily hurt.

In love you expect:
- Romantic courtship.
- Caring attention.
- To share everything.
- To have your dreams and aspirations valued.
- To start a family together.
- Your partner to deal with practicalities.
- Faithfulness, though you may be blind to a lover's infidelities.

How to capture a Piscean's heart
- Make impromptu gifts and romantic gestures.
- Hold hands.
- Use candlelight, flowers and soft music.
- Weekends in Paris, Prague and other romantic places.
- Tell him/her you really love them.
- Take his/her dreams and aspirations very seriously.

FRIENDSHIPS AT A GLANCE

Check here for personality clashes. Friendship matches are not the same as love matches. Think about it: would you actually want to marry some of your friends?

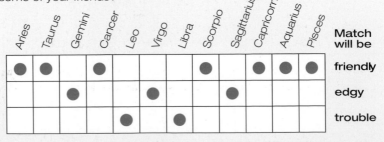

Aries	Taurus	Gemini	Cancer	Leo	Virgo	Libra	Scorpio	Sagittarius	Capricorn	Aquarius	Pisces	Match will be
●	●		●				●		●	●	●	friendly
		●			●			●				edgy
				●		●						trouble

Love matches

Extreme cases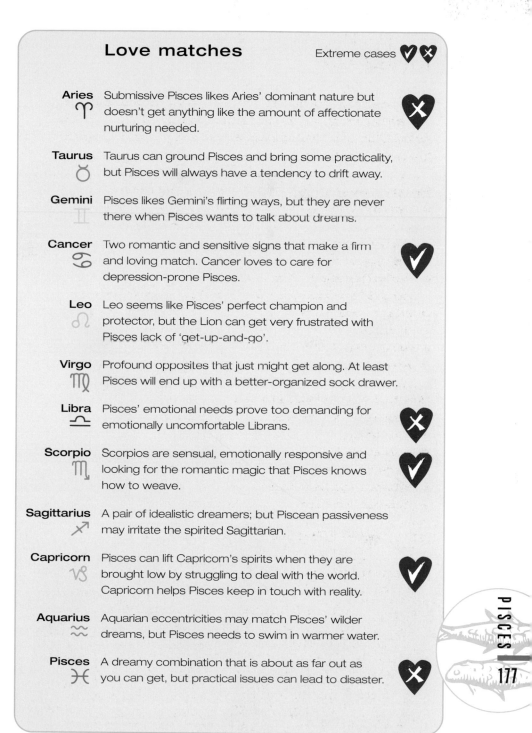

Aries ♈
Submissive Pisces likes Aries' dominant nature but doesn't get anything like the amount of affectionate nurturing needed.

Taurus ♉
Taurus can ground Pisces and bring some practicality, but Pisces will always have a tendency to drift away.

Gemini ♊
Pisces likes Gemini's flirting ways, but they are never there when Pisces wants to talk about dreams.

Cancer ♋
Two romantic and sensitive signs that make a firm and loving match. Cancer loves to care for depression-prone Pisces.

Leo ♌
Leo seems like Pisces' perfect champion and protector, but the Lion can get very frustrated with Pisces lack of 'get-up-and-go'.

Virgo ♍
Profound opposites that just might get along. At least Pisces will end up with a better-organized sock drawer.

Libra ♎
Pisces' emotional needs prove too demanding for emotionally uncomfortable Librans.

Scorpio ♏
Scorpios are sensual, emotionally responsive and looking for the romantic magic that Pisces knows how to weave.

Sagittarius ♐
A pair of idealistic dreamers; but Piscean passiveness may irritate the spirited Sagittarian.

Capricorn ♑
Pisces can lift Capricorn's spirits when they are brought low by struggling to deal with the world. Capricorn helps Pisces keep in touch with reality.

Aquarius ♒
Aquarian eccentricities may match Pisces' wilder dreams, but Pisces needs to swim in warmer water.

Pisces ♓
A dreamy combination that is about as far out as you can get, but practical issues can lead to disaster.

▶ Sex

Romantic foreplay and afterplay are as important to you as the act itself, perhaps more so. Pisceans have a real flair for lovemaking, both affectionate and erotic, and their rich imaginations can produce some wild sexual fantasies.

Your sexuality

For you, sex is very much an expression of love. Your insecurities may make you more promiscuous, though less from wanting to experiment sexually than the need for reassurance of your validity and attraction, and that you have found the right partner. You do not just drop a partner but want to turn the affair into a friendship. If someone breaks off an affair you take rejection very badly.

Sexual needs:

- Being romanced.
- Privacy or seclusion.
- Time to enjoy it fully.
- An imaginative lover, or one who responds to your imagination.
- Constant reassurance of your attraction and desirability.
- Erotic conversation.

Sexual turn-ons:

- Exotic and unusual locations.
- Gentle foreplay rising in intensity.
- Playing out a partner's fantasy.
- Dancing together naked.
- Leather or other clothing with erotic connotations.
- A partner describing what they want to do.

Love and Sex

Although your sensitive nature usually prefers gentle foreplay in comfortable secret surroundings you probably also find sudden advances in unusual places very exciting. Once aroused, your lovemaking can be passionate and abandoned but you need to come down from the heights together.

Famous Pisceans

Date		Person

19 Feb

Prince Andrew
Royal Family,
19 February 1960

20 Feb

21 Feb

Anaïs Nin
Writer, 21 February 1903

25 Feb

Pierre Renoir
Artist, 25 February 1841

George Harrison
Musician, 25 February 1943

27 Feb

28 Feb

Elizabeth Taylor
Actress, 27 February 1932

3 Mar

Linus Pauling
Scientist, 28 February 1901

Alexander Graham Bell
Inventor, 3 March 1847

7 Mar

Piet Mondrian
Artist, 7 March 1872

Liza Minnelli
Actress, singer,
12 March 1946

12 Mar

Jack Kerouac
Writer, 12 March 1922

14 Mar

Albert Einstein
Physicist and mathematician,
14 March 1879

17 Mar

Rudolf Nureyev
Ballet dancer, 17 March 1938

20 Mar

Anaïs Nin
(born 21 Febuary 1903)

George Harrison
(born 25 Febuary 1943)

Linus Pauling
(born 28 Febuary 1901)

Alexander Graham Bell
(born 3 March 1847)

Jack Kerouac
(born 12 March 1922)

Albert Einstein
(born 14 March 1879)

PISCES

179

▶ Everyday life

Pisceans may dream of living in a palace or in a grass hut on a tropical island but the most important thing about a Piscean's home is that it is the place where they are loved.

Your home

You may not normally be a very practical homemaker, apart from the sudden spring-clean or special effort for a particular occasion. Nevertheless, given the chance, you will fill it with imaginative touches. Visitors will find art on the walls, music playing and you will try to offer them good food and wine. It will be an environment where you do not feel bound by a timetable and are free to express yourself.

Your work

Pisceans are best able to overcome their aversion to discipline in caring and creative jobs.

Job for life?

- Actor.
- Dancer, despite its strict demands.
- Artist.
- Advertising.
- Public relations.
- Charitable work.
- Medicine and nursing.
- A religious vocation.

▲ Pisceans (19 February–20 March) are born in the traditional season of relaxation.

PISCES

180

Piscean boss

- Values the unconventional.
- Understands employees' problems.
- Is a good judge of character.

Piscean worker

- Needs an outlet for creativity.
- Needs variety of stimuli.
- Is easily affected by colleagues and surroundings.

Your appetites

Pisceans' imaginative temperaments make them dream of exotic foods, and they love being taken to good restaurants, provided the atmosphere is not too formal.

Your caring nature suggests that you will be happy preparing food for others, though you are not the most practical of cooks. You may well be a vegetarian, in which case the spicy dishes of India and southern Asia will probably appeal. If you bake your own bread you will get great satisfaction from the slow rising of the dough and its transformation in the oven. You probably like the idea of complicated recipes but it is better to keep to the simple ones if you are cooking. You like food presented attractively, and even if you order in a take-away you add a garnish to make it more exciting. Hand-made chocolates are probably one of your favourite tastes.

YOUR MONEY AND YOUR FORTUNE

Economics is not your strong point. You are much more concerned with your emotional and spiritual life than with boring money matters. Follow these suggestions to make your fortune:

- Become a travel agent and help other people get to romantic places (you also have to check them out).
- Become a magician and wave your wand to transform your world.
- Write romantic novels and become a best-selling author.
- Join a ballet company and become a swan princess.
- Stop yourself from buying things you will not use and cannot afford just because they are exotic and interesting.
- Do not lose track of your finances: remember to keep credit card receipts and note cheques you draw.
- Find a millionaire to marry and let them pay for all your fantasies.

Sun-sign tables

If you were born on the first or the last day of the date range for your zodiac sign you should check your birth year on this chart. The Sun moves from one sign to the next at slightly different times each year, so you may in fact belong in the previous or the subsequent sign.

How to read the tables:

- Find the year of your birth and read horizontally across the coloured band until you reach the vertical column for your sign.
- If the date shown is later than your birthday, you were born under the sign in the previous column.
- If the date shown is the same as or earlier than your birthday, you were born under the sign in that column.

Sun-sign table for 1931 to 1941

	Jan Aquarius	Feb Pisces	Mar Aries	Apr Taurus	May Gemini	Jun Cancer
1931	21	19	21	21	22	22
1932	21	19	20	20	21	21
1933	20	19	21	20	21	21
1934	20	19	21	20	21	22
1935	20	19	21	21	22	22
1936	21	19	20	20	21	21
1937	20	19	21	20	21	21
1938	20	19	21	20	21	22
1939	20	19	21	20	21	22
1940	21	19	20	20	21	21
1941	20	19	21	20	21	21

◀ Astrologers have always used complex maps and instruments to produce accurate birth charts.

Jul Leo	Aug Virgo	Sep Libra	Oct Scorpio	Nov Sagittarius	Dec Capricorn	
23	24	24	24	23	22	**1931**
23	23	23	23	22	22	**1932**
23	23	23	23	22	22	**1933**
23	23	23	24	22	22	**1934**
23	24	23	24	23	22	**1935**
23	23	23	23	22	22	**1936**
23	23	23	23	22	22	**1937**
23	23	23	24	22	22	**1938**
23	24	23	24	23	22	**1939**
23	23	23	23	22	21	**1940**
23	23	23	23	22	22	**1941**

Sun-sign table for 1942 to 1964

	Jan Aquarius	Feb Pisces	Mar Aries	Apr Taurus	May Gemini	Jun Cancer
1942	20	19	21	20	21	22
1943	20	19	21	20	21	22
1944	21	19	21	20	21	21
1945	20	19	20	20	22	21
1946	20	19	21	20	21	22
1947	20	19	21	20	21	22
1948	21	19	20	20	21	21
1949	20	18	20	20	21	21
1950	20	19	21	20	21	21
1951	20	19	21	20	21	22
1952	21	19	20	20	21	21
1953	20	18	20	20	21	21
1954	20	19	21	20	21	21
1955	20	19	21	20	21	22
1956	21	19	20	20	21	21
1957	20	18	20	20	21	21
1958	20	19	21	20	21	21
1959	20	19	21	20	21	22
1960	21	19	20	20	21	21
1961	20	18	20	20	21	21
1962	20	19	21	20	21	21
1963	20	19	21	20	21	22
1964	20	19	20	20	21	21

Jul Leo	Aug Virgo	Sep Libra	Oct Scorpio	Nov Sagittarius	Dec Capricorn	
23	23	23	23	22	22	**1942**
23	23	23	24	23	22	**1943**
22	23	23	23	22	21	**1944**
23	23	23	23	22	22	**1945**
23	23	23	24	22	22	**1946**
23	24	23	24	23	22	**1947**
22	23	23	23	22	21	**1948**
23	23	23	23	22	22	**1949**
23	23	23	23	22	22	**1950**
23	23	23	23	23	22	**1951**
22	23	23	23	22	21	**1952**
23	23	23	23	22	22	**1953**
23	23	23	23	22	22	**1954**
23	23	23	23	23	22	**1955**
22	23	23	23	22	21	**1956**
23	23	23	23	22	22	**1957**
23	23	23	23	22	22	**1958**
23	23	23	24	23	22	**1959**
22	23	23	23	22	21	**1960**
23	23	23	23	22	22	**1961**
23	23	23	23	22	22	**1962**
23	23	23	24	23	22	**1963**
22	23	23	23	22	21	**1964**

Sun-sign table for 1965 to 1987

	Jan Aquarius	Feb Pisces	Mar Aries	Apr Taurus	May Gemini	Jun Cancer
1965	20	18	20	20	21	21
1966	20	19	21	20	21	21
1967	20	19	21	20	21	22
1968	20	19	20	20	21	21
1969	20	18	20	20	21	21
1970	20	19	21	20	21	21
1971	20	19	21	20	21	22
1972	20	19	20	19	20	21
1973	20	18	20	20	21	21
1974	20	19	21	20	21	21
1975	20	19	21	20	21	22
1976	20	19	20	19	20	21
1977	20	18	20	20	21	21
1978	20	19	20	20	21	21
1979	20	19	21	20	21	21
1980	20	19	20	19	20	21
1981	20	18	20	20	21	21
1982	20	18	20	20	21	21
1983	20	19	21	20	21	21
1984	20	19	20	19	20	21
1985	20	18	20	20	21	21
1986	20	18	20	20	21	21
1987	20	19	21	20	21	21

Jul Leo	Aug Virgo	Sep Libra	Oct Scorpio	Nov Sagittarius	Dec Capricorn	
23	23	23	23	22	22	**1965**
23	23	23	23	22	22	**1966**
23	23	23	24	23	22	**1967**
22	23	22	23	22	21	**1968**
23	23	23	23	22	22	**1969**
23	23	23	23	22	22	**1970**
23	23	23	23	22	22	**1971**
22	23	22	23	22	21	**1972**
22	23	23	23	22	22	**1973**
23	23	23	23	22	22	**1974**
23	23	23	24	22	22	**1975**
22	23	22	23	22	21	**1976**
22	23	23	23	22	21	**1977**
23	23	23	23	22	22	**1978**
23	23	23	24	22	22	**1979**
22	22	22	23	22	21	**1980**
22	23	23	23	22	21	**1981**
23	23	23	23	22	22	**1982**
23	23	23	23	22	22	**1983**
22	22	22	23	22	21	**1984**
22	23	23	23	22	21	**1985**
23	23	23	23	22	22	**1986**
23	23	23	23	22	22	**1987**

Sun-sign table for 1988 to 2010

	Jan Aquarius	Feb Pisces	Mar Aries	Apr Taurus	May Gemini	Jun Cancer
1988	20	19	20	19	20	21
1989	20	18	20	20	21	21
1990	20	18	20	20	21	21
1991	20	19	21	20	21	21
1992	20	19	20	19	20	21
1993	20	18	20	20	21	21
1994	20	18	20	20	21	21
1995	20	19	21	20	21	21
1996	21	20	21	20	21	22
1997	21	19	21	21	22	22
1998	21	19	21	20	21	22
1999	21	20	22	21	22	22
2000	21	20	21	20	21	22
2001	21	19	21	21	21	22
2002	21	19	21	21	22	22
2003	21	20	22	21	22	22
2004	21	20	21	20	21	22
2005	20	19	21	20	21	22
2006	21	19	21	21	22	22
2007	21	20	22	21	22	22
2008	21	20	21	20	21	22
2009	20	19	21	20	21	22
2010	21	19	21	21	22	22

| Jul | Aug | Sep | Oct | Nov | Dec | |
Leo	Virgo	Libra	Scorpio	Sagittarius	Capricorn	
22	22	22	23	22	21	**1988**
22	23	23	23	22	21	**1989**
23	23	23	23	22	22	**1990**
23	23	23	23	22	22	**1991**
22	22	22	23	22	21	**1992**
22	23	23	23	22	21	**1993**
23	23	23	23	22	22	**1994**
23	23	23	23	22	22	**1995**
23	23	23	24	23	22	**1996**
23	24	23	24	23	22	**1997**
24	24	24	24	23	23	**1998**
24	24	24	24	23	23	**1999**
23	23	23	24	23	22	**2000**
23	24	23	24	23	22	**2001**
24	24	24	24	23	23	**2002**
24	24	24	24	23	23	**2003**
23	23	23	24	22	22	**2004**
23	24	23	24	23	22	**2005**
23	24	24	24	23	23	**2006**
24	24	24	24	23	23	**2007**
23	23	23	24	22	22	**2008**
23	23	23	24	23	22	**2009**
23	23	23	24	23	22	**2010**

189

Need to know more?

There are a vast number of websites that cater to the popular fascination with astrology. Some provide means of drawing up a personal horoscope from which you can devise your own individual predictions. The sites listed here are more informative than most.

This page also includes details of well-established astrological associations as well as some of the most popular journals and magazines in the field.

Astrology Magazines
Culture and Cosmos, PO Box 1071, Bristol, BS99 1HE
www.cultureandcosmos.com
Prediction, Focus House, Dingwall Avenue, Croydon, Surrey, CR9 2TA; tel: 020 8774 0939
www.predictionmagazine.co.uk
The Astrological Journal, The Astrological Association, Unit 168, Lee Valley Technopark, Tottenham Hale, London N17 9LN; tel: 020 8880 4848
www.astrologer.com/aanet/pub/journal
The Mountain Astrologer, (UK distributor: The Wessex Astrologer) tel: 01202 424695
www.mountainastrologer.com

Astrology Societies
Astrological Association, Unit 168, Lee Valley Technopark, Tottenham Hale, London N17 9LN; tel: 020 8880 4848
www.astrologer.com/aanet
Astrological Lodge of London, 60 Gloucester Place, London W1
www.astrolodge.co.uk
Company of Astrologers, PO Box 792, Canterbury CT2 8WR; tel: 01227 362427
The Sophia Project, 60 Ivydale Road, Nunhead, London SE15 3BS
www.sophia-project.org.uk
The Urania Trust, 12 Warrington Spur, Old Windsor, Berkshire SL4 2NF; tel: 01753 851107
www.uraniatrust.org

Astrology Websites
All Free Horoscopes: links to more than 50 free daily, weekly, monthly and yearly horoscopes
members.amaonline.com/liz/default.htm
Astrolabe: free birth charts with several pages of interpretation and PC software
www.alabe.com
Astrology.com: personalized horoscopes, teen astrology, love and relationships and career and money
www.astrology.com
Astrology Online: very detailed sun-sign characteristics and love matches
www.astrology-online.com
Find Your Fate: death, pets', kids' and diet astrologies
www.findyourfate.com
Horoscope-Universe.com: free daily horoscopes plus a large links section
www.horoscope-universe.com
Skyscript: articles, beginner's courses, workshops and seminars, biographies and a forum
www.skyscript.co.uk
Sky View Zone: love matches, relocation astrology and pet astrology
www.skyviewzone.com
Thorsons: wisdom from the Dalai Lama, competitions and books
www.thorsons.com
Zodiacal Zephyr: free birth charts, full sun and moon charts, and celebrity birth data
www.zodiacal.com

Index

INNISFIL PUBLIC LIBRARY

((Collins need to know?

Want to know about other popular subjects and activities?
Look out for further titles in Collins' practical and accessible
Need to Know? series.

A handy one-stop guide
to all the equipment,
know-how and insider
tips you need to take
fantastic digital pictures,
and to store and edit
images.

192pp   £8.99
PB   0 00 718031 4

A practical guide with
clear step-by-step
photography showing
you how to master the
basic skills and
techniques of this
popular game.

192pp   £8.99
PB   0 00 718037 3

An ideal beginner's
guide to painting
landscapes, the
seashore and flowers in
watercolour by three
well-known professional
artists.

192pp   £8.99
PB   0 00 718032 2

A fascinating guide to
all the astrological
know-how on every
sign of the Zodiac and
the characteristics
they are believed to
possess.

192pp   £7.99
PB   0 00 718038 1

Forthcoming titles:
Card Games
Guitar
Pilates
Yoga
Birdwatching
DIY
Drawing & Sketching
Stargazing

To order any of these titles, please telephone **0870 787 1732**.
For further information about all Collins books, visit our website:
www.collins.co.uk